Lifesaving: A Memoir

"In her intelligent, moving memoir, Barrington displays a remarkable clarity about the years when she, recuperating from her parents' accidental deaths, went off to heal herself in Spain and become a young woman. The author is especially shrewd about the erotic education of her younger self. But what makes this memoir so refreshing is its unillusioned (as opposed to "disillusioned") perspective and wry, dry humor. There is not a trace of self-pity anywhere. The prose is unostentatious and utterly trustworthy; the narrator, excellent company for a voyage of discovery/self-discovery."
—Phillip Lopate

"Beautifully written. . . . The picture she draws of the small town in Catalonia is vivid, sensuous, not just the scenery magnificently created but the daily life of the town, the people she meets. . . . The writing is spare, precise, poetic when it needs to be. This is the recollection of wild youth from the perspective of a wiser and more integrated mature self, but she does not interfere with our perceptions of her at nineteen. She gives us her adventures, the chances she took, the luck that carried her through danger . . . never attempting to depict herself as victim or to manipulate us into pity."
—Marge Piercy

"Throughout her writing is superb; she evokes smalltown Spain under Franco in lush detail with solid philosophical insight into the tragedy that changed her life. . . . Among the growing number of memoirs, *Lifesaving* is a gem."
—*Publishers Weekly* (starred review)

"*Lifesaving* is about a life once again saved in and by a writer's memory."
—PEN/Martha Albrand Award for the Art of the Memoir

"Landscape, culture, character and language—all come alive under Barrington's deft hand and sumptuous eye. Intimate in detail, this beautifully conceived memoir is psychologically astute and honestly written. A brave self-portrait and moving journey of a daughter's search for her self."
—Dorianne Laux

"*Lifesaving* reminds us that memoir is an art form, and can equal the novel in shapeliness, intensity, and fascination. Barrington's easygoing narrative and the good humor of the tone—often disarmingly funny—conceal a dark, driving undercurrent of pain. The complex levels of imagery build to a resolution as hard-won as it is inevitable. It's not easy to be honest about one's youth, about the lies one's lived, about death, about sex, but that's what this story is about, and it's told with a beautiful honesty. I think a great many people will find it speaks to them about the hard places and the hard choices, while they love it for its sunlit picture of a woman young, wild, and wildly alive."
—Ursula K. Le Guin

Five Books of Poetry

"Barrington's history, like Lowell's, is intensely personal; her geography, like Bishop's, extracts the familiar from the exotic and the exotic from the familiar."
—*The Nation*

"Barrington's sharp, bifocal vision gives me nearby and distant physical and emotional domains and holds them to a light I've not seen them in before."
—*The Kenyon Review*

"In Judith Barrington's striking collection . . . human emotions come ushered and accompanied by animal companions, especially the horses this speaker loves. Here they are witnesses, companions to the spirit, and as vulnerably mortal as human beings. Socially and politically alert, lamenting and celebrating, Barrington's passionate poems inscribe the broad range of her affections."
—Mark Doty

"Judith Barrington's new book of poems is informed by a strong sense of time and place: the specificities that reify human interchanges for tellers and hearers of tales. There are powerful stories here: the death of a child's parents by shipwreck; a twenty-year-old's unnameable affair with a woman of forty; even a lover's allergic reaction to a bee sting fuels a vignette of confrontation with mortality. In many poems, a formal framework inspires a reader's assurance and fascination with this writer's craft and direction: she knows where she is taking us—Gibraltar, Scotland, Oregon, sites of some of her well-lived lives—and we want to go with her as, on the way, poet, lesbian, grown woman in a world at risk, she gives the unnameable a plethora of names."   —Marilyn Hacker

"'The poem,' writes Judith Barrington, 'has lodged in my heart like a stone in the shoe.' It is the perfect image for recollection. Here are the horses of her English childhood and the outbreak of World War II filtered through family reminiscence, her coming of age, the disastrous marriage and her self-acceptance as a lesbian. In the brilliant, excruciating title poem, undercover investigators watch but do not interfere as killers break the leg of a racehorse; the poet seeks to understand how savagery can coexist with intellectual detachment. When the crowbar strikes, she asks, what happens to the human soul? Her voice is lyrical, her intelligence palpable throughout this book."
—Maxine Kumin

"*History and Geography* is traversed by a keen avenue of sound sense, a confidence of detail, and a rich, often difficult landscape of experience which Judith Barrington calmly, courageously explores. I am moved and fortified by the sense of healing litany in this work, particularly in the poems to her parents. The prose memoir, 'Fish,' swims luminously alongside, helping define the vast borders of a compassionate, generous life."   —Naomi Shihab Nye

VIRGINIA'S APPLE

Books by Judith Barrington

Nonfiction
Lifesaving: A Memoir
Writing the Memoir: From Truth to Art

Poetry
Long Love: New and Selected Poems, 1985–2017
The Conversation
Horses and the Human Soul
History and Geography
Trying to Be an Honest Woman

Virginia's Apple

COLLECTED MEMOIRS

Judith Barrington

Oregon State University Press   Corvallis

Oregon State University Press in Corvallis, Oregon, is located within the tradi-
tional homelands of the Mary's River or Ampinefu Band of Kalapuya. Following the
Willamette Valley Treaty of 1855, Kalapuya people were forcibly removed to reserva-
tions in Western Oregon. Today, living descendants of these people are a part of the
Confederated Tribes of Grand Ronde Community of Oregon (grandronde.org) and the
Confederated Tribes of the Siletz Indians (ctsi.nsn.us).

Library of Congress Cataloging-in-Publication Data
Names: Barrington, Judith, author.
Title: Virginia's apple : collected memoirs / Judith Barrington.
Description: Corvallis : Oregon State University Press, 2024.
Identifiers: LCCN 2024030466 | ISBN 9781962645225 (trade paperback) | ISBN
    9781962645232 (ebook)
Subjects: LCSH: Barrington, Judith. | Poets, American—20th century—Biography. |
    Poets, English—20th century—Biography. | Lesbians—Spain—Biography. | BISAC:
    BIOGRAPHY & AUTOBIOGRAPHY / LGBTQ+ LCGFT: Autobiographies. |
    Essays.
Classification: LCC PS3552.A73647 Z46 2024 | DDC 811/.54 [B]—dc23/eng/20240710
LC record available at https://lccn.loc.gov/2024030466

♾ This paper meets the requirements of ANSI/NISO Z39.48-1992
(Permanence of Paper).

Oregon State University Press
121 The Valley Library
Corvallis OR 97331-4501
541-737-3166 • fax 541-737-3170
www.osupress.oregonstate.edu

For Ruth

A NOTE TO READERS

Each of these memoirs was originally written as a story complete unto itself. For this collection, I ordered them to make one longer narrative, editing to avoid repetition and allowing characters to reappear without introduction. Because of this, *Virginia's Apple* may offer a richer reading experience if it is read in order from the beginning.

CONTENTS

THE WALK HOME

ROY WAS a landmark. Everyone who had cause to walk or drive or ride the number twelve bus up or down Tongdean Lane noted his presence just before the narrow, sooty tunnel under the railway that led to a sports stadium enclosed by an S-bend on the hill.

Roy's house, outside which he sat, thrashing around uncontrollably in his wooden wheelchair, is gone now. It was the last one on the right before the tunnel—a bungalow squatting at the foot of a grassy embankment along which trains clattered, some headed for London sixty miles to the north, others almost arrived at Brighton, a few miles down-rail. Today, Tongdean Lane is lined on both sides with tall office buildings that have turned the corner from the main road, where for several decades they have welcomed drivers to Brighton with their boring facades of brick and glass. Large notice boards announce that these not-quite-skyscrapers are home to insurance companies and consultants of nebulous varieties, whose names reveal nothing of their purposes. The buildings have an abandoned air about them, even though someone must come to trim the grass and shrubs between the low brick walls that serve as landscaping.

Tongdean Lane was quiet back in the 1950s, too, when my family moved to the neighborhood. Then it was an inhabited quiet that I walked through on my way home from school—the quiet of a street where mostly old people lived and could occasionally be encountered pruning a rosebush or, with their feet in fluffy slippers, walking a popeyed dog on a leash. My bus, the number 5, didn't turn up Tongdean Lane but continued along the main road towards Patcham. There was, however, a convenient bus stop right on the corner, so I could jump down, say goodbye to my friend Tisha, who lived on the other side of the highway, and begin the trudge up the hill, swinging my satchel filled with homework and novels in which teenage girls and their ponies were the heroes.

The day we moved over to this part of town from the old house in Portslade—the only time we ever moved—I was eleven and had managed to catch the flu. It might, in fact, have been a reaction to leaving the only home I had ever known. There is loss involved with such a move; but in that era, in the world I knew, such things were not acknowledged. I was pretty sick by the time school let out, and completely forgetting about the move, I caught my usual bus to the old neighborhood and walked wearily up the long hill (why did we always have to live up hills?), only to arrive at the shell of a house that was no longer home. Somehow, perhaps through the kindness of a neighbor, I got word to my parents, who picked me up and took me to the new house. There I lay in front of a smoky coal fire, wrapped in a quilt, until my bed arrived in the moving van. I was tucked into it and left to recover, which I did by morning.

The next day, I got it right and took the new route home. The minute the bus pulled away, I heard Roy starting to shout. Over and over, the same garbled words, interspersed with long pauses, forced their way out as his head rotated or fell back and his arms windmilled furiously. This first encounter with Roy somehow merged in recollection with the previous day's fever to become a slightly uncomfortable memory. He came into my mind just before I fell asleep, his voice croaking as he spluttered and called out, his wrists doubled over like hairpins, as if a dreadful cramp was tugging them into impossible shapes.

It was his oddness, I suppose, that I was afraid of in the beginning—or was it really fear? I remember being more bewildered than anything else as I walked on the left side of the road, pretending to ignore his repeated shouts: "What's . . . yooooor . . ." followed by a lot of swallowing and head rolling, until he produced the final, triumphant, ". . . name?" His inability to muster his words and take charge of his limbs provoked a kind of discomfort I had never felt before, and a desire to pass by as quickly as possible.

In those days, disabilities (a word not yet in circulation) were never discussed, at least not by people with no professional connection to them. My school had nobody who wasn't able, both physically and mentally, and I had never come across anyone, child or adult, who was what might have been referred to in hushed tones, as ". . . you know." I didn't figure out until much later that Roy suffered from cerebral palsy; adults, including my mother, referred to him as "a spastic."

After about a week of ignoring him, I realized he was going to be there whether I liked it or not, so I crossed the street, looked him in the eye, and answered his daily question.

"Hello," I said. "My name's Judy."

After that, I always walked up his side of the street.

"Alloo-oo-oo, Joo-oo-dy," he would manage after several false starts, and as I got closer, I would see a grin stretch his face as a gurgle of pleasure rolled around his throat. It soon became clear to me, without having to think about it, that he was completely *compos mentis*—that the only impediment to our conversation was his inability to control his lips and tongue and throat, which, refusing to cooperate, went their own ways, like his legs and arms.

Sometimes I would stop beside him as he struggled to ask if I was on my way home from school, and occasionally I volunteered information: I told him I was going to a movie that my mother had forbidden, or what a disgusting lunch had been forced down our throats that day. Other times, particularly after the routine had been established, I resented his expectations and was short with him, muttering, "Hallo, Roy," and walking right on past the wheelchair as his head fell forward onto his chest in an attitude of despondency, which I pushed out of my mind as I turned past the sports stadium and headed for my tea.

Autumn darkened into winter, and my walk grew more solitary. There were only a couple of streetlights in the lane, and nobody except Roy was ever outside. It was after five o'clock when I got off the bus, sodden leaves muffling my footsteps. Curtains had not yet been drawn across lighted living room windows; inside, a man would be sitting with his feet up, reading a newspaper, or a woman would be bustling around, engaged in some early-evening task. Sometimes an orange cat dozed on a windowsill, or the still rare flicker of a television made me think about the weekly serial *The Cabin in the Clearing*, which I was watching on our new set. These nights, I looked forward to Roy's greeting, and when he wasn't there, the street seemed unfamiliar, even spooky. He rarely sat out in the rain, although sometimes his mother forgot to wheel him inside in time, or perhaps she didn't notice the weather until his old green sweater was steaming slightly in the yellow pool of light from the bridge lamp.

It never occurred to me to ask him questions. How old was he? The normal clues for age didn't seem to apply, and, indeed, I never even wondered. Now, I think perhaps he was in his twenties. His face was deeply lined, but that might have been from the effort everything took—the scrunching of muscles, frowning and tightening at each attempt to speak or smile or stay still. His eyes, I do remember, were a startling bright blue, and he was very thin. Had he been able to stand up, I think he would have been tall, though he was barely able even to sit straight and was usually slumped over the bar that held him in his chair, his feet waving about above the metal footrests.

That winter, he started dropping his keys a lot. I don't know why he was entrusted with a bunch of six or seven keys, but as I plodded up the hill, he often held them in one waving fist, his fingers pressing them hard into his palm. When I was close, the keys would drop or fly away with an unplanned swing of his arm. Laboriously, he uncurled his fingers and pointed with one of them, often not the index finger, in the general direction of the keys. The tone of his request was clear, if not the words themselves. "Okey-dokey," I would say, an expression I had learned from the new TV set, and pick up the keys for him.

It was a still, dark night the first time he grabbed my wrist as I handed the keys back to him. His grip was painfully strong, and the tips of his fingers dug into my forearm as he pulled me down onto his lap, the bar that held him into the chair pressed into his stomach between us. I had only a vague feeling of doing something wrong, although I do remember being on the lookout for his mother, who might emerge at any minute to fetch him in for his tea. My navy blue school tunic was rucked up and my bare legs felt warm on his brown corduroy trousers. It was an unfamiliar sensation, but not an unpleasant one. I stayed there for five or perhaps ten minutes, while Roy's body subsided into an unusual calm. Once in a while, an arm would shoot out and from time to time, his hand clenched around the wheelchair bar, but mostly he just sat there, his tongue protruding a little, his eyes smiling happily as his head swayed from side to side.

It seems strange now that I didn't obsess about this encounter, which turned into quite a habit over the next few weeks, but I didn't think about it much at all. It was simply something that happened on the way home—something slightly naughty that I could get away with when I wanted, even though I still had days when I brushed him off abruptly, not wanting to go through the ritual of the keys and the lap that night.

Then one cold and slightly drizzly Friday, when I was later than usual because of a lacrosse practice, Roy tried to tell me something different. "The keys," he said, pointing to his side and bending his vowels until I grasped the word. "Po-cket," he managed, pointing again.

"You want your keys out of your pocket?" I asked.

"Yeah!" he exclaimed, nodding violently, his head arching back till his chin was in the air and then whistling down onto his chest.

So I put my hand in his pants pocket to find the keys.

I remember the feel of the pocket's rough cotton as my fingers moved across his thigh. And I remember the shock when I encountered his steel-hard penis, just, of course, as he had intended me to. I snatched my hand out, blushing and confused, and marched on up the hill without saying goodbye. The next evening, Roy's mother was standing at the gate, her arms folded across her plump breast, looking businesslike. Surely he couldn't have told her? I greeted them both politely and walked on.

His mother hardly ever appeared after that, and I continued to sit on his lap when no one was around. How did I explain to myself the willingness with which I groped in his pocket for those keys, half-repulsed and half-fascinated by the anatomy I bumped into as if by accident? And why did I shy away as if in shock when his unruly hand managed to clamp down on mine just as it touched the crucial spot inside the pocket? It was as if I was willing to put myself in the danger zone but wasn't going to do anything once I got there. And I didn't.

Sometimes, it seems now that I should be ashamed, not of the small sexual explorations, but of the ease with which I stood up and left him. Indeed, there were times he appeared so depressed on a day following one of my abrupt departures that I was forced to admit, just for a moment, that I might be treating him unfairly. And yet, I tell myself defensively, he was a grown-up, and he had started it. Of course, if he had not been in a wheelchair, I would have felt terrified—the way I was terrified when other men did inexplicable sexual things: the old man on the bus whose pants all of a sudden revealed what I didn't want to see, leaving me paralyzed and silent; the blue-blazered man in a standing crowd at Wimbledon who, in the midst of an exciting first-round match, placed his penis right in my bare hands, which were clasped behind my back. These men left me feeling furious and guilty, even though I had no choice in the encounters and was not in any way to blame. With Roy, I had made a choice; I was at least partially responsible for the continuing flirtation between our bodies—his sinewy, male, and out-of-control; mine preadolescent, long-legged, and curious. But I never felt the same disgust that I associated with the men I thought of as perverts.

It bothers me now that I failed until much later to consider Roy's life. I never wondered what he did all day when I wasn't walking home from school, how he took a bath, whether his mother read to him, or what radio programs he liked. And what happened to both of them later, when the bulldozer razed the street to make way for some financial services group? At that time, there were few resources for someone like Roy. His mother must have been dedicated; yet some days she surely resented the demands of her severely handicapped son. Did he end up in an institution when she couldn't go on or when she died? Did he die young? Or is he somewhere still, waving those arms around, better medicated, better entertained, no longer stuck outside all day to watch the passing traffic?

As it happens, some five decades later I own a handicap parking sticker, having been diagnosed with a neuromuscular disease that is gradually impairing my mobility. Even if I eventually end up in a wheelchair—which I might—there's absolutely no way I can compare my own disability with Roy's, the memory of which has finally come to wrench my heart. I make a point of talking confidently about my situation, of yelling at people who steal the disabled parking spaces I rely on, and of demonstrating that there is no indignity in walking with a cane or running out of energy before the party is over. It was the shame, back in the fifties, that made it impossible to ask my mother about Roy—impossible almost to think about him.

What comes back with the greatest clarity is the intense blue of his eyes and the surprising sweetness of his smile as he plotted his difficult moves. My biggest regret, these many years later, is that I was too young, too scared, and too paralyzed by unexplained guilt to lift up the wooden bar, put my head on his bony shoulder, and snuggle into his body until our breathing merged, our heartbeats slowed down, and we were both quite still.

THE CONDOLENCE DOG

APPARENTLY, THE Battersea Dogs Home in London, like so many shelters, had plenty of lurchers. Which may be why in January 1964, a large, brown, energetic, and untrained lurcher appeared in the upstairs apartment at 99 Lexham Gardens. When I opened the front door there it was, standing on long elegant legs, sniffing amongst the dust bunnies underneath the furniture. At the sound of the door closing, a pair of green eyes fixed on me and a stringy tail gave a tentative wag.

We were four tenants, two of them my friends, Joanna and Lydia, whom I'd met when we shared a previous flat. They had proved as anxious as I to get away from the bossy woman whose name was on the lease, so the three of us scooped up a fourth unanchored young woman and ended up in this roomy top floor.

When, the following month, my parents drowned in the *Lakonia* cruise ship disaster, leaving me to contend with becoming a nineteen-year-old orphan, neither Jo nor Lydia could handle it. Shielded by protective middle-class parents from the "loss" of pets or relatives, they had been well schooled in the denial of death. Their level of discomfort was such that on finding themselves alone in a room with me, they suddenly remembered an urgent errand. Looking back, I'm certain they wanted to help me—that their sympathy was real—and perhaps that was where their urge to get a dog came from; somehow it replaced the words that refused to come together in their mouths as phrases and sentences. They simply couldn't say them out loud.

Of course, I was just as inadequate as they were when facing the awful possibility of a conversation about death: an excruciating awkwardness overtook us all. Overnight I had become someone quite new—someone touched by a disaster that would be a constant source of embarrassment to my friends. It was humiliating—almost as if my parents' deaths and the social dilemma they provoked were my fault. Thus, I became consumed by guilt when I should instead have been consumed by grief.

My mother and father had gone away for Christmas—a decision that shocked my older brother and sister. They weren't quite sure how to explain it to themselves or to other people, but over time a story emerged: Mother and Father had grown weary of planning Christmas in a way that would satisfy both families and their young children. Surely, they had left in order to avoid the haggling of previous Decembers.

For me, though, it hadn't been an issue. I had no yen for a family gathering. I was living the high life in London, partying every night, and going home to Brighton for the weekend occasionally to use Mother's washing machine. No need to worry about me, I'd assured the parents; in truth I'd much rather stay in the city. So I was at a hair salon preparing for the festivities when my brother tracked me down to tell me the cruise ship, heading south towards the Canary Islands, had caught fire. For the next several days, I stayed with his family, where my sister and her children also came to wait for news.

Later, with the ship still on fire and Mother and Father still missing, I rushed back to my job as junior secretary to the head of artist bookings at the BBC, where they were extraordinarily kind. They gave me a direct phone line to television news at Alexandra Palace, which brought me the most up-to-date bulletins about what had, by then, become a worldwide news story of an international rescue effort to pick up passengers who, like my parents, had been forced by the fire into the ocean. Women in my department invited me to dinner at their homes and the personnel department offered me compassionate leave for as long as I wanted, but I didn't want their leave: I just wanted to continue living my new, grown-up life with its glamorous job at Television Centre. I loved leaning casually against the doorpost, chatting to Dusty Springfield, eyeing her hairstyle and false eyelashes, and opening the door for Harry Belafonte who sashayed in to pick up my boss for a lunch date at The Ivy. That was reality: the disaster was only a dream.

ONCE PASSENGERS were picked up by ships—from lifeboats or the sea—it took a long time for that news to make it back to those of us waiting. No one was called personally, there was simply a recorded message, with names of survivors added throughout the day. One day, unable to tolerate the not-knowing, I went to the company's headquarters, determined to find someone who would talk. But when I arrived at their offices just off Regent Street, I found myself in the midst of a crowd of black-clad, wailing Greek women—mothers, wives, or perhaps widows of crew members. They were expressing their pain in a mixture of traditional Greek laments and British outrage, but they were being ignored. Not a single Greek Line representative appeared on the front steps—no publicity person with a rehearsed speech in hand—not even a nervous secretary to reassure the sorrowful throng.

At a later time in history, we family members of the drowned, as well as the surviving, traumatized passengers, would have been understood to need professional help. But even before we could learn the fate of our loved ones—whether snatched from the ocean and carried to safety or drowned and their bodies picked up by a rescue vessel—the Greek Line was carefully ignoring us.

Soon I was sent home from the office to be with my family. We all sprawled in my brother's sitting room, bickering politely about who was next in line to brave the cupboard under the stairs, where the old-fashioned, black telephone squatted among cleaning supplies. One of us, I'm not sure who, had just been in there, crouched under the sloping ceiling that was covered with phone numbers scrawled in pencil, and had dialed the shipping line again, only to return looking glum and repeating: *no change*. It was then that my sister Ruth leaned forward with a shudder, as if to wake herself from the trance induced by that recorded list of survivors' names that, by then, we all knew by heart and hated. She leapt to her feet, bursting into furious organization: Did I have the phone number of Mother's cleaner? Who was taking care of the dogs and did that person have a key to the house? Were the beds made up? What about spare blankets—they must be put in the airing cupboard right now to be warmed for Ma and Pa's return. And because she led the way, we were all, very soon, eagerly awaiting their return.

Another afternoon, perhaps that same one—those days unfolded in a haze—Ruth burst out with a new idea, again interrupting our descending mood. We were getting worn down by the television helicopters' pictures of our parents' holiday vessel swathed in smoke and ringed by ships unable to get close. It was now apparently up to Ruth again: she must buck us up, jerk us out of resignation, and pack the room, wall to wall with belief.

"Think about it," she urged, leaning eagerly into our circle, making eye contact with us, one by one.

"We've all been out sailing with Pa, haven't we? Think about it. Go on . . ."

But we remained sluggish, slumped over.

"The reports—that last one on the telly," she went on, her voice almost shrill. "Listen to me! They said there was debris floating around."

My brother opened his eyes and stared at her.

"Well, come on now: think about that debris; what does it consist of?" A pause. "Remember the Kon-Tiki . . . rafts . . . think about lashing boards together . . ."

We were all looking at her now. Had my sister gone completely bonkers?

"Our father can do that," she concluded triumphantly. "He's working on getting them home. And, what's more, that's what he's doing right now!"

But that's not how it turned out. In time, their names were added to the list of the dead—the most definitely dead—and all that was left for Ruth to do was to drive down to Brighton and pick up Sara and Piccola, Mother's beloved dachshunds.

NEITHER LYDIA nor Jo offered any explanation for the sudden presence of the dog in our flat. I picked up the idea that it was their plan to "cheer me up" or at least to keep me busy, since I'd reluctantly agreed to take the compassionate leave that everyone seemed to think I needed. Perhaps it was simply an instinctive act of genuine kindness.

It was probably Lydia who came up with the name, Fred. She and Jo both found its solid, working-class thump hilarious, and fancied themselves walking around well-mannered South Kensington shouting, "Fred, Fred, where are you?" while collapsing into someone's hedge in a fit of giggles. We were, after all, nowhere near as grown up as we liked to think.

"Remaining in place furtively"—the derivation of "lurcher" from Middle English—turned out to be one of Fred's skills. For a creature who dashed around so madly, he was able to hold himself surprisingly still, lurking like a shadow, with only his eyes catching the light. One night, I took him out just before closing time, and he rushed off along the Cromwell Road, swerving in through the doorway of a friendly local. When I pushed open the door, he stayed poised, quite motionless, until he ducked round my legs and bolted up the alley that led to the outside toilets. He moved deftly to one side and popped into the Gents, where he stayed for some time before I was able to entice him out. I can only imagine what the regulars thought of a young woman hovering outside the Gents, hissing, "Fred . . . come out, come now, damn you!"

The archaic meaning of "lurcher"—prowler, swindler, petty thief—was also lingering in Fred's DNA. Once I took him into Tesco (in those days, dogs were more welcome in shops than they were later) intending just to run in and buy some noodles. I spoke sternly to Fred, who began looking around in amazement at so much stuff. Glancing sideways like a hardened pickpocket, he ducked, doubled back under his leash, and whisked it out of my hand. Then he was off, his ears flying comically as he galloped up and down the aisles, trailing the long, leather strap, which flew up and lashed the legs of several shoppers. With relief I saw him heading towards the exit doors, but unfortunately, he had to make a sharp turn at the end of canned foods. Some Tesco employee had spent an hour or two that afternoon building a shoulder-high pyramid of Heinz soups on special offer. Fred skidded on his large paws, like Nadal sliding up to a drop shot on the red clay of Roland-Garros, and made the turn easily. His undoing was the leash that took a shortcut through the base of the display, causing several hundred cans to crash noisily to the floor and roll away in every direction.

EVEN THOUGH my flatmates had brought Fred home for my benefit, I never for a moment regarded him as my dog or my responsibility. Between us, we remembered to feed him adequately, and took him out for boring walks from which he did his best to escape. Still, we all agreed never to return him to the Dogs Home.

The truth is I can't remember his face. I remember Fred only as a loose-limbed creature (part greyhound, part something else, as all lurchers are), one soft ear pointing up and the other pointing down, unresponsive to commands and always unhappy indoors. Through no fault of his own he was no sort of companion through those early days of unacknowledged, unimaginable loss.

After a month or two, Jo and Lydia realized it was hopeless: Fred was never going to cheer me up. Possibly they noticed that I never talked to him, nor he to me. Certainly, I would never be transformed into a cheerful country girl, striding around in Wellington boots with a faithful lurcher at my heels.

"Fred's leaving," Lydia announced. "My mother's found a friend to take him. They have a farm near Lindfield."

"Okay," I said, hardly glancing up from *To the Lighthouse*, through which I'd been struggling since the New Year. At this point, I was more than a little in love with Mrs. Ramsay.

And then Fred was gone.

NICOLETTE

MY FAMILY always hated Nicolette, but my mother hated her most of all.

It started in 1955, when Nicolette waltzed into the lives of my Uncle Guy and Aunt Joan—a woman my mother adored—and rapidly disappeared to Italy with my uncle, breaking up a thirty-year marriage. (I was ten, and nobody talked about it in my presence, but I heard plenty, just the same.) Underneath my mother's outrage at the divorce and at Nicolette's "shameless" behavior, lay other, less legitimate complaints about the interloper: she was flashy and overdressed; she smoked untipped cigarettes in a holder; she had married two different men before Uncle Guy—indeed, she commanded way too much attention from men; and, worst of all in the eyes of my British family, she was *foreign*.

Her history was murky. She was the daughter of an Italian count— no, she came from humble origins in the Aosta Valley. Mostly she spoke with a not-quite-perfect upper-class British accent, but sometimes she rolled her *r*'s or threw out phrases in French or Italian. Then for a while, her English would become redolent with the Mediterranean, until she remembered that Guy was a retired brigadier and her army-officer-wife voice would return. The mystery surrounding her origins irritated my mother, who insisted she must have something to hide. For me, though, listening behind half-closed doors, the mystery was tantalizing. By the time my mother finally agreed to let Nicolette and Guy come for a brief visit, they had been married for four years and I was fourteen. I felt as if Grace Kelly had been invited to tea.

It started badly. The couple arrived early and my mother, flustered, emerged from her bedroom after my father had taken their coats. Sweeping into the hall, Ma glanced at the oak chest on which our glossy black cat, Banjo, liked to sleep, and swiped at it. "Get off, you naughty cat," she hissed, sending Nicolette's mink stole flying away into the kitchen. Nicolette let out a peal of laughter, delighted by this piece of farce, though my mother retreated, mortified, and remained unusually silent the whole afternoon. Nicolette had the upper hand, but, wisely, she didn't overplay it.

She quickly grasped that I was the only member of the family who could be charmed (my father and brother were both vulnerable but on too tight a leash), and so she devoted her exclusive attention to me. I took her to the music room and sat at her feet while she listened to my favorite records, asking me grown-up questions that no one had ever asked before: "Have you seen any interesting plays lately?" and "Don't you just *adore* that new Ella Fitzgerald record?"

A few weeks later, a letter arrived from Italy inviting me to stay with them. "Absolutely not!" said my mother, and that was that—for a while.

FIVE YEARS later my parents were aboard the *Lakonia* when it caught fire off the Canary Isles. By the time their fate was established and their bodies were identified, I was badly in need of distraction.

Wouldn't I like to go back to Wales with her for two weeks? Nicolette asked when she telephoned to say she was coming to the memorial service. She and Guy were renting a ramshackle old lodge near Llandyssul. My emotions grew wild and confusing when I heard her voice on the phone.

"Your uncle is too ill, darling. He won't be coming with me. I'll represent him to the family. He was so terribly fond of your mother, you know. He's quite devastated."

Though Guy had never seemed to care much about his brother, he had, indeed, been keen about my mother, who was, in turn, attached to him, despite my father's irritation at his profligate lifestyle. Whenever my uncle had visited, he usually managed to request a loan, without any chance of success. He once planned to invest in ponies he thought he could resell to polo players in the Aga Khan's orbit. He and Nicolette had been moving in circles way beyond their means.

Was he really ill, or, as I detected from some hint of satisfaction in her voice, was Nicolette just looking for a chance to escape by herself? She readily agreed to stay the night at my London flat before going down to Brighton with me. Then, she said, we would drive back together to the Welsh hill country.

At Paddington Station, people hurried down the platform but there was no sign of Nicolette until, as the crowd dispersed, a first-class carriage door flew open and she appeared. The way I remember her is with a drink in one hand, cigarette holder in the other, slowly descending the steps in her fur coat and high heels.

"Ah, there you are, dearest Judy!" she said, kissing the air close to my cheeks, and exuding a strong aroma of champagne. "Oh, you poor child. I just don't know what to say."

"Don't you have any luggage?" I asked, anxious to change the subject. "I'll get a taxi."

She gestured back to the carriage, where a short man in a camel hair overcoat with a velvet collar was handing down suitcases to a porter.

"Mr. Sherman says he'll take us to your place, darling. It's right on his way to the Dorchester. Such a dear man! We had a delicious chat on the train."

Mr. Sherman turned out to have a Rolls Royce waiting in the forecourt of the station, which delivered us to my untidy Lexham Gardens flat. Neighbors peered through their windows as the chauffeur carried

Nicolette's case and bags up the three flights of stairs. Mr. Sherman whispered something and handed her a card, then winked at me before jumping back into the Rolls and cruising off towards Knightsbridge.

Later, after she had changed her clothes and tried, unsuccessfully, to engage me in conversation about the *Lakonia*, she settled by the gas fire with a large scotch, leaving me to throw together a meal. While I fussed around in the kitchen, she threw out remarks about my parents.

"It's all so horrible to think about . . ."

"Don't you wonder what they must have gone through . . ."

"Your dear mother was so sensible. Your father too. They must have given way to other people. It would be so like them . . ."

The clink of ice cubes.

Then, in a tearful voice, "Oh, you poor, poor child!"

"Dinner's ready," I said. "I hope you don't mind eating in the kitchen."

She pushed the food around her plate and drank a good deal of wine before, quite abruptly, she said she was sorry but she had to go out for a while. It wasn't until I heard the downstairs door slam that I thought to ask when she'd be back. I ran to the window, but it was too late; she was climbing into a taxi.

For a while I wandered around the flat, switching on the old, flickering TV, then turning it off impatiently. Finally, picking up a book someone had left on the couch, I tried to read. My flatmates were away and it was strangely silent as I turned the pages, occasionally getting up to make instant coffee. Around eleven, I started to feel both worried and tired. Where on earth could she be? We had to leave early in the morning to drive to Brighton for the service.

By midnight I was furious. She had no key, so I couldn't go to sleep. Anyway, I had no idea where she was or if she was all right. I told myself that she was forty years old and could damn well take care of herself, but I didn't believe it. I looked up the Dorchester in the phone book and dialed the number.

"Mr. Sherman, please," I said, hoping I sounded forceful.

"I'm sorry he's out," said the desk clerk. "I don't know when he'll return."

"Listen," I said with as much authority as I could muster. "It's extremely urgent that I contact Mr. Sherman. Do you have any idea where he went?"

"Well," said the clerk hesitantly, "He did say he could be reached at Crockford's if anything important came up."

I ran downstairs and knocked on the door of the flat below mine, where four young men lived. I knew Tom was staying in town for the holidays and prayed he might be home. He appeared in his pajamas, rubbing his eyes.

"I'm desperate," I said, tugging at his arm. "You've got to put on a dinner jacket and take me to a posh gambling club in St James's."

"Okay," he said, sleepily. "When do you want to go?"

"Now!" I said. "Immediately. Go and get dressed."

The uniformed parking attendant looked askance at our old blue van but let us pull up in a corner. Taking Tom's arm, I explained to the host that we were with Mr. Sherman. We were escorted along a red-carpeted hallway into the gambling room where the murmur of conversation blended with the click of the roulette ball and the *faites vos jeux* of the croupiers. My hair was a mess, my shoes were scuffed, but Tom was elegant in his bow tie. I scanned the crowd and spotted her at the far side of the room, perched on a stool halfway along a table with Mr. Sherman standing beside her, his hand with its large, gold signet ring lying on her shoulder.

He seemed not at all surprised to see me and shook Tom's hand in a friendly way. Nicolette told me she had won a lot of money. Indeed, there was a pile of chips in front of her.

"Well, cash them in," I said abruptly. "We're going home now."

Again, Mr. Sherman was not surprised. In fact, he seemed rather relieved. When she descended from the stool, I realized why he was so agreeable about handing her over: she was almost too drunk to stand up. Smiling amiably, she took one step, lost her balance, and stumbled against the table. Piles of chips collapsed onto the green baize. Tom leaped forward and caught her round the waist. Heads turned in our direction as we took her by the elbows and walked her between us out to the van. Mr. Sherman never even said goodbye.

The next day, I sat stoically through my parents' memorial service and then gathered with the family at my sister Ruth's. Only one memory lingers with perfect clarity: I am in the kitchen; Ruth and I are scraping bits of potato and fatty roast beef into the garbage.

"I know you're going up to Wales with Nicolette, but if you like you can stay here instead," Ruth says briskly, without looking at me. I turn to see if she means it, but she is concentrating hard on the leftovers. She hasn't stopped for a moment since we got back to the house and looks determined not to breathe for several days.

Whatever I thought—and I didn't think about it for more than a second—I was well past resisting the mysterious promise of Wales. That night, I drove to Llandyssul, straight through the bitter January darkness, with Nicolette dozing in the passenger seat. What would have happened, I will wonder over the years, if I had decided, instead, to put her back on the train and wave her out of my life?

For the next two weeks, I spent most of my time sleeping, drinking, and writing notes in response to hundreds of condolence letters. Several times, we went out for lunch with people Guy and Nicolette knew, and once they made me dress up and go with them to the Tivyside Hunt Ball. Disconnected images from one or another of those days have stayed with me—my uncle tall and jaunty with his neat moustache and a flamboyantly dotted, yellow bow tie; Nicolette blond and sharp-nosed with her legs elegantly crossed.

One day, Nicolette and I walked along the river path at the bottom of the water meadow. Beside the swirling river, muddy with rain, we stopped and turned towards each other. When our eyes met, I felt a charge surge through me.

Then, at Easter, she invited me back. I arrived after another grueling night drive in a rainstorm, winding along the narrow lanes that follow the rivers and flying into the air from humpbacked bridges. When I finally arrived, I discovered she had sent my uncle away to visit his son. We had the house to ourselves.

Death became a formidable presence there in Llanfair Lodge, where I refused to talk about my dead parents, refused to cry, refused to acknowledge that anything at all was wrong. In spite of my denial—or perhaps because of it—death surrounded us as Nicolette and I fell into bed together. It beat, along with the rainstorm, against the old window panes as she placed my hand on her breast and whispered into my ear what her body wanted from mine. It crammed itself into the corners of the room and entered me. I didn't know that it would never go away, no matter how deeply I lusted, no matter how desperately I loved.

At the moment I felt her legs wrap around mine, I panicked, throwing off the quilt and bolting into my clothes and down the stairs. I started the car and drove furiously down the lane. Rain had soaked the mossy banks until new springs overflowed across the slick surface. I skidded in a half circle, ending up with my back wheels in the ditch.

For a few minutes I just sat there, the car making those faint creaks and groans it makes after you switch off the motor. Then I got out into the downpour and walked around to the back. I could barely see the wheels in the dim red glow of the lights masked by sheets of falling water, but they appeared to be buried in mud. The nearest farm was half a mile back up the lane; I could hardly wake up the farmer to tow me out of the ditch at this hour. Anyway, I would have to walk past Nicolette's to get there—walk right past the house with its bedroom light still glowing and Nicolette waiting there in her silk nightgown and a bottle of brandy by the bed.

I stood very still as water seeped through my clothes and dripped off my eyelashes and nose. No dog barked. No owl hooted. There was only steady rain, sloshing into the puddles on the one-lane road and drumming on to the leaves of the beech trees that grew along the bank. My stomach growled: a yearning and a terrible fear threatened to spill over into obscure but overwhelming joy. I knew I wasn't going to do anything about the car: perhaps I had intended all along to go back to the house, even if I hadn't ended up in the ditch. Hadn't this dash for safety been a sham?

Even out there in the wilds of Wales, Nico, as I started to call her after that night, had found her way into the social life of the county set. We moved from cocktail party to cocktail party, interspersed with an occasional dinner at someone's home or a pub lunch with a group of rowdy farmers. In between, there were the nights, which stretched out long and warm, filled with words of love mouthed from lips to ears, while slow caresses and sudden urgency built into a rhythm that merged with the cries of the spring wind that rattled the windows.

One afternoon, we walked down the lane from the lodge. To our left, water meadows, dotted with sheep and crossed by the meandering lane with its single-arched bridge, slanted down to the river and rolled on towards the village. To our right, the valley rose steeply through beech woods. Without speaking, we turned and scrambled up on a firm bed of dirt. Tree roots snaked along the ground and, in spite of the weak sun glancing through the foliage, it was dark and otherworldly. Nico wheezed asthmatically as we climbed, pausing now and then to catch her breath. As the ground leveled out and the trees thinned into a high meadow, we came to a fence over which five ponies hung their heads, nickering softly as they saw us, and snuffling into my hands when I reached out to them.

"Sorry, no treats!" I said, as Nico rubbed necks and kissed soft pony-noses. Watching her, I was overwhelmed with longing. She looked up and met my gaze. Silently, we moved back into the trees and sat down. Two curving roots embraced an oval hollow in which we lay together, the warm wind licking patches of briefly revealed skin as we made love there, letting out soft murmurs of appreciation and muted groans of excitement that blended with the rustle of the leaves and the munching of the ponies.

That evening, I felt important and protective when I drove Nico to a party, the slightest hint of sunshine giving me an excuse to put down the hood of the green convertible I had so recently inherited from my mother. I wanted to squire her into the high-ceilinged square rooms with their chintzy sofas and sporting prints—to hold her hand possessively as we threaded our way through crowds of men in dinner jackets and women in little black dresses, and to hold the car door open for her when we left in the small hours of the morning. But we acted as lovers only in private; in public we were strictly aunt and niece, a pretense about which I complained from time to time. When Nicolette snapped, "Well, what exactly do you imagine we could do?" I would mumble something about running away to a desert island. Then a wave of distress would surge up my spine as she turned away with a shrug: "Don't be so ridiculous, darling."

"This is my niece, Judy," she would say, after kissing our hostess poutily on both cheeks. Then, dramatically lowering her voice, "She lost both her parents in the *Lakonia* disaster . . ." I would blush and turn away to find a waiter or a young man who could supply me with a large whiskey or a champagne cocktail. As I wandered away, I'd hear Nico extolling the virtues of my "poor dear mother," and telling the gathering crowd just how "absolutely ghastly" it was for me. I was mortified and tried to pretend it was someone else she was talking about, despite the glances that came my way as she warmed to her story.

There was always a gathering crowd. At parties it was a group of men who clustered around her, their expressions closely mimicking those of my father and brother, wide-eyed and slightly befuddled, but eager, that first afternoon Nico had come to our house. At the shops in Llandyssul, it was a crowd of whoever was handy. Even before she went into the greengrocer's or the bakery, the royal manner in which she strode along the village street caused a stir of attention—some of it slightly hostile, but most eager to follow her inside. Sometimes she told and retold the story of my sudden bereavement, but often she simply requested or supplied a piece of local gossip.

"Gladys up at the farm has . . ." here she looked around and stepped closer to her audience, "her *nephew* from South Africa visiting, you know." And, even though this same nephew had visited many times before, Nico managed to provoke in her listeners a very real doubt that he *was* Gladys's nephew, raising the specter of family secrets too awful to imagine.

Towards the end of my stay, I noticed that Nico herself seemed to have a lot of secrets. From time to time, she would ask me to drive her into the village and leave her there for an hour, with no explanation of what she was up to. The first time this happened, the morning after a particularly passionate night of lovemaking, I got it into my head that she was going to buy me a surprise present, but when I picked her up, she offered nothing and was oddly silent as we drove back along the lane by the river. Every few days, a white van would pull up by the garage and a man in a sheepskin coat would haul out a big box and go round to the back door. Whenever Nico heard the van, she would frown and say, "wait here a minute," hurrying to the kitchen as the man knocked. Once, I followed her a few minutes later and found her standing on a chair, putting away a bottle of scotch on the top shelf of the china cupboard. "I said *wait*," she snapped. So I turned away, hurt as I was so often hurt by her changing moods. It wasn't until more than a year later that I grasped the full extent of her drinking and began to find the bottles she hid all over the house. By then she was buying from a village further away, her line of credit having dried up in Llandyssul.

As our affair unfolded, I hid from everyone the fact that I was involved with a woman, but still my flatmates and friends picked up that something was going on. I had no outlet for my euphoria and, like anyone in love, I longed to shout it all over town or, at the very least, to confide in one person. At the same time, I couldn't think about Nico without being enveloped in a cloud of shame. After a while, my mixture of exhilaration and reticence led my friends to conclude I was having an affair with a married man and I let them believe this, while I lived with the terror that the truth might come out. I muttered under my breath when I talked to Nico on the phone, afraid that someone would overhear. I rushed to the mail in case anyone noticed how often I got letters with that same sloped handwriting and a Welsh postmark. Discovery, or even suspicion, I believed, would bring about the end of the one thing that wholeheartedly engrossed me, the one thing that was keeping the images of my drowning parents at bay and my precarious life afloat. In fact, I pretty soon began to consider ending that life. Fantasies of suicide frequently followed bouts of solitary drinking.

Somewhere during this time, I found myself feeling quite ill and taking refuge with my old school friend, Sue, who lived in Earl's Court with a group of young women, all training as nurses. I slept on their couch at night and lay there wordlessly during the day, while they tiptoed around and offered soup. Now and then I heard them discussing me, fragments of their theories floating in and out of range.

". . . he dumped her, did he?"

". . . someone I've never met . . . no I don't know where . . ."

I curled up and covered my head with a blanket. Wrapped in the warm darkness of the wool, I wondered what Nico was doing and I shivered as I realized she was probably drinking and flirting with anyone she could find. Several days later, I walked back to my flat, took my clothes to the launderette, and returned to work. The personnel department of the BBC continued to be sympathetic and my boss hardly seemed to notice my absences. Being the department head, he had two secretaries, but barely enough work for one.

One night in November, my flatmates and I threw a party that quickly became packed with drunken acquaintances and strangers, all dancing to the throbbing pulse of the Beatles. "Love, love me do," we bellowed in unison, and "roll over Beethoven." The floor was bouncing and someone in the building called the cops, who were quickly absorbed into the party, passing round their helmets and knocking back cheap wine with the rest of us. Sometime later, a new policeman came in, his serious expression noticeably out of synch with the room. He grabbed one of the dancing cops and muttered into his ear, then, looking around, located the record player and cut the music. The room was suddenly silent, but still vibrating, as he asked for our new flat-mate, Kylie, who stepped forward, her tumbler of wine trembling in her hand. She was led out and the news ran around the room. A bad accident down the Earl's Court Road: her younger sister, a fifteen-year-old, had been taken to the hospital. The parents had asked that Kylie be notified.

I looked around. Several women who knew Kylie were crying and the guys were shifting uncomfortably, not sure what to do. I turned to the record player and twisted the volume control. "Ple-e-e-eeze, love me do-oo," pleaded Paul and John as I made for the brandy bottle in the kitchen. Nobody's tragedy, not even my own, could touch me. I could no more cry over a sweet young woman fighting for her life than I could reveal my heart to my best friend. My heart had become a wilderness where all I could see was Nicolette; my dead parents were still hidden in the tangled undergrowth.

I SAW my family less and less. Much as I would try to avoid the subject of Nico, she was too juicy a topic for them to ignore. My brother or sister would say, "Heard the latest?" and I'd be pulled into uneasy solidarity, joining them in their disparagement of the woman only I knew was my lover.

Aunt Joan was particularly bitter. It was close to intolerable to chat with her over a gin and tonic in her studio, surrounded by canvasses and the smell of linseed oil, while the secret of my liaison with the woman who had stolen her husband loomed so large and so close.

When I was a child, Joan, my godmother and favorite aunt, had often invited me to stay at the farm in Devon where she and Uncle Guy had lived for some thirty years. There was a dangerous bull to keep clear of, and calves from the Jersey herd to bottle feed. I'd reveled in roaming the thatched house, the beech copses, and the rolling fields through which they both rode their thoroughbred hunters.

Joan had a deep, gruff voice and wore tweed skirts; when she walked, her toes pointed out a bit like a duck, which I found both comic and endearing. She was a serious artist; some of her work is in the National Gallery. She also painted portraits of horses—often the winner of a big race, posed with its ears pricked and its jockey immaculate in his owner's colors—for which she was highly paid, although she hardly needed to earn a living. My only wealthy relative, she had inherited plenty of money. When not painting, she would stomp amiably around the house and garden in the only shoes she ever wore: Hush Puppies, which she purchased in bulk once a year, making a special trip by train to London for the purpose.

When Nicolette had swanned in with her designer shoes and her Je Reviens perfume, Guy had traded in the bucolic life (and his wife) for swinging Italy. But Joan remained irrevocably connected to my family and to important moments in my life, like the red-letter day when, at twelve, I finally achieved my ambition to own a horse. She met Mother and me in Castle Combe, where a friend of hers had a likely young horse for sale. In her brown hacking jacket and jodhpurs, she trotted round the ring on Black Magic, leaning forward as if to study his gait or commune with his twitching ears. Mother and I stood with the owner in the middle of the school, the two of them making conversation while I eagerly watched horse and rider. Magic was beautifully groomed, even down to some neat patterning on the gloss of his hindquarters; his hoofs had been oiled and his tail pulled to narrow neatness. When Aunt Joan stopped rising to the trot and dug her seat into the saddle, using her legs vigorously, he broke into a canter and circled first one way, then the other. We could all see that he tended to lead with the same leg in both directions, but our hostess was reassuring. "He's young," she shouted, so that Joan could hear. "He'll learn quickly."

Joan, preparing to pop him over a couple of hurdles, nodded her agreement. Then, the hurdles safely negotiated, she came to the center and patted Magic's neck heartily as she dismounted. "I think he'll do," she said, and I felt myself rising up from the dirt, flushing red to my ears, and beaming stupidly as if I would never stop.

Aunt Joan had even gone with us one summer to Spain, setting up her easel in the riverbed to paint the old village of Caldetas—a peaceful scene of a horse and cart, dozing at the siesta hour, which now hangs in my Oregon dining room. Her luggage consisted almost entirely of painting supplies—no swimsuit, just the familiar tweed skirt, despite the heat. That summer, I remember constant laughter between Joan and my mother, the two of them suntanned, relaxed, and swapping discoveries about the history of the region. Now, with my parents suddenly dead, Joan stepped up, invited me to her new home in Kent, and began depositing a small monthly allowance in my bank account.

It wasn't just the living remnants of my family who demanded my loyalty. My mother had been adamantly opposed to allowing Nicolette into her home; how could I reconcile that with my constant and painful longing to have Nico in my bed—to have her as far inside my body as I could get her? Everywhere I turned, I betrayed someone: when I was with Nico, it was the family I was deceiving, and when I joined the fold of the family, I denied not only Nico, but also my own deepest feelings. Prevarications began to flow through my veins as naturally as the blood, which occasionally flooded my face, threatening to betray the fragile balance I had struck between all the unspeakables that made up my life.

NICOLETTE AND I were still lovers when, despite knowing that it would be torture to be separated from her, I quit my job at the BBC and went to work at Perelada Castle in Spain as a tour guide to the wine cellars and castle. Even while I was still in London, our encounters had been furtive and infrequent, our contact mostly limited to long, expensive telephone calls, each of which I faithfully recorded in my diary with a series of cryptic initials. Now, living in Figueres, just over the border from France, I was alternately enchanted with the nightclubs and beaches of the Costa Brava and smitten with headaches and loneliness. I went through each day forcing myself to appreciate the warm shaft of sun that struck me as I emerged from my hotel and walked to the café for morning coffee. I tried to conduct my tours of the castle with genuine interest in the people who came, and I threw myself into sudden friendships with Dutch families and Spanish bull-fighters, driving over the mountain to water ski at Llansá or smooch with a waiter in Rosas. But often I would wander across the *rambla* in the mellow heat of early evening to place my calls to Nico at the *telé-fonos* building, where I usually had to wait for several hours before the connection was made.

Sitting on a hard bench opposite the two telephone booths, I would chat with other would-be callers—women keeping in touch with hus-bands who worked away from home or with parents back in some village. Outside, the traffic hooted and roared, children screamed, and donkey carts rattled over the cobbles. I leaned against the whitewashed wall, rehearsing the words I would say to Nico when finally the clerk called my number. Several times a week, too, I wrote her intense letters and received, in return, letters which I chose to read as equally intense, but which I later realized she had crafted so that they might seem to an outsider merely the words of an affectionate aunt.

One day in August, weary from the relentlessly cheerful groups of tourists I had escorted through the wine cellars, I arrived back at my modest hotel on the square to find an airmail envelope with Nico's handwriting. I took the stairs two at a time, tearing open the letter as I burst into my room. It was 6:30 and still hot, so I threw open the shutters, letting in some evening light and the noise of the street three floors below, where people shopped and chatted or shouted from window to window across the alley. Sitting on the edge of my iron bedstead, the frame digging into the back of my thighs, I pulled two folded pages from the blue envelope.

"Darling Judy," she wrote, "I must go to Italy in two weeks' time to deal with some financial matters." She went on to explain that, in addition to the money that her father had left her—long-since spent—she had also been left a half share of his home in the village of Luserna San Giovanni: "A house that I have loved my whole life," she wrote, "a house that I must now sell, even though it will break my heart in two." The problem was, she said, that her father had left it jointly to her and her sister, Gully, with whom she did not get along. Desperate for money and needing a break from the boredom of Wales, Nico had planned to meet Gully in Italy to negotiate a deal. "My darling," the letter ended, "won't you drive over and meet me there. You will be such a help. I can't manage without you."

It wasn't exactly a quick drive across town—it was some five hundred miles from Figueres to Turin along winding roads and over mountain passes—but I didn't hesitate. My busiest weeks as the winery's tour guide would be over by then. Even if my employers didn't agree, I would go. After all, *she couldn't manage without me.*

I drove flat out for most of two long days in the Triumph, which I still thought of as my mother's. With the top down, I crossed into France after a three-hour traffic jam at the border, skirted the Camargue and Marseilles, and cruised along the Grande Corniche.

In the early days of what already felt like a doomed affair with Nico, I had wandered one evening into the Gate Cinema in Notting Hill and caught Anthony Perkins and Melina Mercouri in *Phaedra*, a modern version of the Greek tragedy. I'd returned the next evening to watch again, stunned as Perkins fell to the floor in front of the blazing fire with his glorious stepmother and then, later, drove the Aston Martin, which she had given him, off the edge of the Grande Corniche to the accompaniment of Bach's Toccata in F. Now, heading for Italy, I played that scene over and over in my mind. Like Tony, I was in the grip of a forbidden obsession. Like him, I felt the urge to sing out loud, turn the wheel towards the road's edge, fly off the cliff and fall to the rocks and the crashing waves far below.

I spent the night at a grubby inn in the foothills and the next morning set off for Turin, where I had arranged to meet Nico at a hotel at six o'clock. It was ten to six when I ordered myself a vermouth at the bar, after cleaning up and changing in the faux-marble restroom off the lobby. I was not particularly surprised when six o'clock passed and then seven o'clock and eight o'clock. Nico was never on time. But still, as I ordered drink after drink, and ate all the olives on the bar, I felt panic rising. Then, soon after 8:30, she bustled in.

"Judy, darling!" she said. "We got held up, but I knew you'd be here." She waved a hand towards the man and woman who had quietly followed her in. "This is my old and very dear friend, *carissima* Santina, and her adorable husband, Sergio."

I shook hands with Sergio and Santina, immediately liking them both, although I ached to be alone with Nico so I could tell her how horrible the months had been without her. Nico insisted that we all sit at a table for a drink before heading back to their home in Ivrea where she had arranged for us to stay.

Over the next few days, between stolen moments of lovemaking in Sergio and Santina's spare room, or parked in a gateway outside the village of Luserna San Giovanni, I listened, understanding only a word here and there, as Nico and Santina talked about people they had known growing up together. I played my role as Nico's helpful niece, while in our room, divided by a thin wall from our hosts' room, our furtive lovemaking continued.

La Fontana, the disputed property, was an ivy-covered villa with a peaceful, overgrown garden and, of course, a fountain dripping from stone ledge to stone ledge, where the gravel paths intersected near the front door. On the appointed day we wandered around for half an hour or so, Nico dabbing her eyes with a handkerchief and muttering to herself, before Gully showed up in a rented Ford. She was utterly unlike Nico; the only thing I recognized in Gully that I had also encountered in her sister was a ruthlessness, which boded ill for the negotiations.

Gully didn't want to sell the house: she preferred to buy out Nico's share. Although I had only just turned twenty and knew nothing about property or Italian law, they both seemed happy to use me as a go-between and advisor. That first morning, the three of us talked in the garden over the hum of bees and insects, the tranquility of the place occasionally disturbed by Gully's impatient exclamations and Nico's exaggerated anguish. The next day our meetings moved indoors; chairs were dusted off and papers strewn over a rosewood table. Nico wanted to retain some visiting rights, but Gully wanted to be done with her. Anyway, they couldn't agree on a price. Hours were eaten up by digressions into who had taken what from the bedroom drawers or the kitchen cupboards and which sister had been favored with more gifts as a child.

When I suggested leaving the two of them alone, Nico insisted that I stay. Frequently she would flare up at Gully: "I need a break from this. I'll be back in an hour," and she would take my arm and guide me to the car so I could drive her down the street to the village bar, where she would knock back a few brandies. Sitting in the *taverna*, a cave with whitewashed walls, she would relax, tossing her head to laugh with the locals and shouting out witticisms, which she sometimes translated for me. Sooner or later, she would grip my arm tightly.

"Oh Judy, Judy!" she would moan. "It's my father's house, where I grew up. Oh *dio, dio*! That woman should not end up with it!" And she would wipe her eyes with a floral handkerchief and put her lips close to my ear.

"I love you so much," she would say. And I believed her.

Although this visit, like so much of my time with Nico, was fraught with melodrama, there were also moments that put the whole careening affair into stasis. Each morning, I sat on the ottoman next to the dressing table in our room, watching Nico cleanse her face and put on her makeup. This was something I had done in Wales, where she used to sit at the triple mirror in the bay window, looking out over the sage and gray valley. As she wiped the cream off her skin, her face emerged with a naked vulnerability. At first, this had scared me: I didn't know this demure, ordinary woman and I wasn't even sure I wanted to know her. But here in Italy, when she bared her face and caught my eyes in the mirror, I felt a familiar surge of protectiveness. She sighed, reached for a cigarette, and began to paint on her face. Years later, I would think about that so rarely exposed skin and realize that not only the face mask but the alcohol and the whole gamut of her behavior, like mine, was geared to burying desperation.

Six days after the rendezvous in Turin, I took Nico to the airport. We had reached an agreement with Gully, renewed our secret life, and, as usual, were about to go our separate ways. I wasn't looking forward to the eighteen-hour drive back to Figueres, nor to the busloads of visitors I would ply with champagne for another two months before I could return to England and see Nico again. Longing to throw myself into her arms and kiss her, I tolerated, instead, her "aunt and niece" display as she kissed me on both cheeks and held my hands in hers. Her perfume, for a moment, drifted around us both.

"Thank you darling," she said, already turning towards the gate. And then, almost over her shoulder, she called, "You've been an angel. Where would I be without you?"

IT ENDED when I became involved with another woman. At first, this new development threatened to break through my denial about what I was doing: falling in love with one woman could be an aberration, but doing it twice surely meant something. For a long time I had been, at least with men and by the hypocritical standards of the time, a "good" girl as far as sex was concerned. But now, with a second woman, my life seemed no less than doomed. I was presented with a grim vista of the future: I would forever be skulking in unsavory places. I'd never have friends I could talk with openly. And my awful secret had a name, although it was a name I refused to allow anywhere near my vocabulary.

I didn't consciously think any of this but it was, nevertheless, a consuming package of terrors that reached its height when Nico came to London to visit some old friends and demanded that, on her last evening, I meet her for dinner. Afterwards, driving her back to the station to catch the night train to Wales, I stopped under a tree along Birdcage Walk and cut the engine.

Turning to face her in the dim illumination of a streetlight, I blurted out, "I've fallen in love with another woman and it's your fault. You've turned me into a lesbian."

It was the first time I had uttered the word, which had, it seemed, been in my vocabulary all along. Nicolette recoiled as if I had struck her. There was only the ubiquitous rumble of big-city life as I glared at her, burning with indignation, and she shrank away, briefly silenced by the power of that word we both so dreaded.

"Now, Judy darling," she began finally, reaching a gloved hand out towards me, but I interrupted the speech I knew was coming. I didn't want to hear how she was sure I would meet a fine young man and that this was just a difficult time for all of us—whoever "all of us" were. "I'm taking you to the station," I said.

MORE THAN eight years had passed since the Wales days. I'd been married and divorced, and Guy and Nico were living in Wiltshire, renting another in a long line of country cottages attached to large estates. This time they were enjoying their proximity to several market towns, which meant for Guy some new horsy acquaintances, and for Nico a selection of pubs and off-licenses where she could buy on credit. I called and said I'd like to come down to see them. Nicolette seemed delighted and offered lunch.

It was a spring Sunday when I drove past Marlborough and turned into a tree-lined driveway that stretched away from the stone pillars at the turnoff. After a while, the drive curved around to a sweep of gravel in front of the mansion. Following Guy's directions, I skirted the great house in my purple Mini and bumped along a grassy track to their cottage, where I ducked my head through the doorway and found the two of them preparing a haphazard meal. Nico was far from sober. I tried not to recall all those nights when she had passed out and I had undressed her and put her to bed; the time she had fallen down the stairs; the sickness and the maudlin tears. I adopted the cheerful pretense that all was well as I settled down to chop carrots.

Uncle Guy sat in a kitchen chair, his long legs in ragged trousers sprawled across the flagstones, telling me about the local trainers; racehorses, he said, were big around here. Now and then he would shout affectionately at Nico, still using his habitual endearment, derived from an insulting term for foreigners that apparently didn't bother her.

"Get a move on, Woggy! We'll all starve to death if that joint doesn't go in the oven soon."

It wasn't until after 3 o'clock that the three of us sat down to roast leg of lamb, amply flavored with rosemary, and unintentionally blackened roast potatoes. When we finally cleared away the plates, Guy wandered off to take a nap, while Nico and I moved into the shabby sitting room.

"I've wanted to tell you," I began, but Nico, sensing the approach of something she didn't want to hear, interrupted me.

"Let me make some coffee," she said, and hurried into the kitchen. When we sat down again with the little Italian coffeepot between us, I said firmly, "It's about that night in London."

Nico looked nervous, but laughed and said, "Go ahead, go ahead! You young people are so insistent with your speeches about things!"

"You remember, when we stopped in the car and I told you that you had turned me into a lesbian."

Nico shifted uncomfortably.

"Well," I said, "I want you to know two things: first of all, I would've been a lesbian even if I'd never met you. You didn't make me one. And second, I'm not sorry about it anymore. In fact, I'm glad."

Nico sipped her black coffee, which, judging from the smell, had a large shot of whiskey in it, and looked at me speculatively.

"But you must get married," she said at last. "I know it didn't work out the first time, but you can always try again. You can't live with women all your life."

"Of course I can," I said, annoyed at how out of touch she was with the feminist world I had so recently discovered.

"But Judy," she pleaded. "At least find a man who'll turn a blind eye."

I locked eyes with her, forcing her to wait for my response. "I'll be fine." I said firmly.

Nico went to the kitchen and poured herself another drink. I started to get out of my chair to follow her. I wanted to convince her, but the slightly sweet smell of alcohol lingered in the air and I knew that Nico wasn't going to be glad for me, no matter how hard I tried.

WHEN I turned fifty, my friends, who were organizing a big party for me, solicited written memories from people to put together in an album. Nicolette's name was on the list I compiled and my friend, Phyllis, sent her the request. Nico replied to her by return mail:

Dear Miss Oster,

Thank you for your communication of the 4th May.

I don't know that I would call myself "Friend of Judith Barrington" but I am certainly her aunt; I am the widow of her paternal uncle, Guy Barrington.

Judith stayed with us for a time at our home in Wales, after the tragedy of her parents' death. After that we did not see much of her—she went to the United States not long after. I enclose a not very good photograph of her at that period. Please give her my good wishes and congratulations on her achieving her half-century on the 7th July.

Yours sincerely,
Nicolette Barrington

Over the years, I'd heard news of her, usually through my brother who felt an obligation to keep in touch with the widow of our father's only brother. Once in a while, I'd received a communication from Nico herself, letting me know how well she was doing. She'd gone through a bout of shock therapy, which she told me had erased all her memories of the years in Wales. There had also been several periods of drying out and, later, scraping together a living as a companion to a series of old ladies, she got into AA and gave up drinking. I didn't hear about it when she was finally hospitalized for the emphysema that all those cigarettes had left her with, but I did get news of her death.

For thirty years I'd gone back and forth, never quite sure what version of our story to settle on: sometimes I felt sorry for her, fragments of the old tenderness fluttering alive in my memory, but more often I was furious at her for taking advantage of me at that most vulnerable moment in my life. She was twenty years older than me, as well as my aunt, and the stories of incest survivors, unleashed into public view by the feminist movement, resonated strongly during my angry years. By allowing our bond to become sexual, she certainly hadn't "turned me into a lesbian," but she had isolated me from any possible source of support, while proving quite incapable of helping me find a path into the grieving I denied for so long. What's more, her homophobia had put its stamp of approval on my own.

And yet—at nineteen I was not a child. I'd been reckless in my pursuit, wooing her with long-stemmed roses and love letters. I'd driven five hundred miles for a chance to light her cigarettes. I'd rolled around crying with laughter when she spun a wicked tale about Gully or imitated the stuffed shirts at some dinner party. I couldn't deny the triumphant joy I'd felt at flexing my own seduction muscles for the very first time.

I RARELY think of Nicolette now, but Llanfair Lodge, with its silent rooms, planted among muted green hills and drystone walls, has taken up permanent residence in my imagination. When I think of it, I am prowling restlessly indoors, seeing again the views from upstairs. Outside the house I can breathe the cold, mountain air, but inside, the smell of alcohol, together with the constant hum of sexual longing, fills the air, obliterating the creak of the stairs, the clatter of willow-pattern plates, and all conversation. Whiskey bottles crouch in cupboards or behind books and, over and over, the record player churns out "Autumn Leaves" and "*Non, je ne regrette rien.*"

Twenty-five years after I first went to Llandyssul, my partner Ruth and I were on holiday nearby when, on a whim, we turned off the highway, drove through the village and up the lane to the lodge. Between hedges thick with Queen Anne's lace, my hands and feet took over. Steering and braking in a pattern they remembered well, I negotiated blind corners and swerved into turnings without looking at signposts, until we came quite suddenly upon the old place with its reddish beams crisscrossing the front wall. There was a small B&B sign in the front window. We lingered there, gazing at the river and fields that bordered the quiet valley. Everything was still except for the haphazard wanderings of distant sheep and the flurry of a passing crow. Then we drove on, the unspoken question filling the car until finally Ruth said, "What would you think about spending the night there?" I stopped the car in a gateway and we sat mulling it over. "Is that a good or a crazy idea?" I didn't know, but I wanted to do it.

Inside, the house looked different, but the new paint and bright furniture somehow made me remember even more clearly the old, worn carpets and peeling wallpaper. The good cheer of the young owners contrasted sharply with the melancholy of those long-ago tenants. And when we went upstairs to our allotted room—the very room where I had waited for Nico night after night—the view from the upstairs landing through the stained-glass window was startlingly familiar. Later, lying in bed, I knew by heart the pattern of the blackened ceiling beams.

About two in the morning, in the pitch dark, I crossed the room with three unhesitating strides and climbed the four narrow steps to the bathroom. It wasn't until I was back in bed that I realized how instinctively I had turned my bare feet sideways on the narrow stairs because I knew that they would stub my toes if I took them head on; and how I had sat down on the toilet in the dark knowing exactly where it was. On the way back, too, I had reached for the door handle with its iron thumb latch, and placed my hand directly on it with no fumbling or groping.

Long ago I'd made that same trip to the bathroom and returned to bed in that same room to wait for Nicolette, who belonged in another bed in another room. There, with the beams overhead, I had learned about the pleasures of the body, about deception, and about the whine of inexorable guilt. Every day as dawn brought a subdued light to the window, I looked out at the hills and wished I could escape. Yet when I walked away from Llanfair Lodge across the fields, I would turn and look back at it—and then, from a distance, I would love it. As even now, I still do.

THREE ARUM LILIES

I'M NOT sure how I talked myself into marriage. I had fallen in love with a string of women after the affair with Nicolette, but I was still resisting the obvious. Indeed, I'd created such an elaborate cover involving numerous boyfriends that my family had started to describe me as "boy crazy." For a while there were three named Martin—not all at the same time, although there was some overlap. What I liked most about these men was the sense they gave me, in those first years of my twenties, that I was succeeding at being the kind of young woman I was supposed to be. But I wasn't wild about any of them until Colin came along.

He was more appealing than the others with his long, reddish sideburns and a taste for black shirts with light ties that made him look rakish. His sense of humor, his rebelliousness, and his enormous horse, Frank, all drew me into his circle—a group of upper-middle-class, country people with long-established habits, where he fit only marginally. It's clear to me now that he was in as much danger of not belonging as I was.

We were introduced by mutual friends at the tennis club, although Colin was not really a tennis club type. Wearing bright colored T-shirts and dirty gym shoes on the manicured lawns of the Grasshoppers

Club, he slashed at the ball with an untutored but effective forehand. Sunday afternoons we sat side by side on the grass, drinking tea and smiling at the white-clad members who ran to the net exclaiming "well played, old chap" or chased a ball to the baseline with "I say, what a good shot." Slowly, as he warmed up to me, he revealed that his mother had wanted him to follow in his dead father's footsteps to become an army officer, but he had refused. I could see that he wouldn't have done well as a soldier, having little appetite for following orders or even suggestions. So—for now, he said—he was working with a friend to build up a smoked fish business in a Sussex village at the foot of the Downs.

That he had a dead parent never struck me as a point of connection; not once did I ask about his father—not even how he had died—and although Colin knew of my parents' deaths, he never asked me about them either. Looking back, I can see that his fatherlessness must have played a role in the independence I recognized and liked. He was attentive to his mother, but she wasn't a factor in the decisions he would make.

He shared a home with his brother Roddy, whose business was renovating old houses. On a quiet country road, a short walk from the brothers' favorite pub, Roddy had restored the house with traditional red Sussex tiles. The outbuildings included a large barn for Frank where, among bales of straw and old farm implements, the seventeen-hand-high chestnut munched his hay with one or other of the bantams perched on his back.

Colin spent his workdays chugging up and down little rivers in an outboard dinghy, putting out and hauling in homemade eel traps. Smoked eels were a popular, expensive delicacy and the fledgling business was making good money from them; he was saving the cost of flying them in from Japan—or so he said. Actually, it seemed to me that he just enjoyed puttering up and down those waterways. He was a free spirit of a kind I'd never encountered before.

I still didn't know him very well when he invited me out for dinner in London on a day when he paid his regular visit to Billingsgate Fish Market to buy trout and salmon for the smoker. We met in Queen Anne's Gate near the Albert Hall, an elegant avenue where I could leave my car for the evening. Colin arrived in his battered green van, leaped out, and, after greeting me shyly, proceeded to change his trousers in the street while I pretended he had nothing to do with me. Moving off, the passenger seat wobbled alarmingly and its unruly springs dug into my behind. As I turned to fiddle with the seat, I noticed two hay bales in the back.

"Supplies for Frank?"

"No. It's to get rid of the smell of fish."

There was no answer to this, since I was already wondering whether the overpowering stink would make dinner out of the question. As we cruised along Knightsbridge, I felt more and more nauseated. Staring out at the self-satisfied mannequins in Harrods windows, I tried not to breathe, but it was no use. Just as I was considering asking Colin to stop, I noticed a movement at my feet and what appeared to be a snake emerged from under the seat.

"Good Lord!" Colin said. "I thought I'd lost that big one. Sorry. I'll just move it into the box." He stopped the van, picked up the eel and put it away behind the hay.

We ate dinner at one of the French bistros ubiquitous in the late sixties, with red checked tablecloths and candles perched crookedly in Mateus Rosé bottles grown into waxy stalagmites. After steaks and crème brûlée, Colin asked if I'd mind a quick stop on the way back to my car.

"Arsenal played today," he said, as if that explained it.

So we spent half an hour parked outside a television shop, while Colin watched the end of the match. At this stage of the relationship, I found such habits rather endearing.

In spite of a life full of boyfriends, parties, and casual sex, it had been a long time—more than five years since my parents died—without any genuinely carefree moments, and Colin had a gift for joy. I still have a snapshot of him dressed in pink jeans and a sky-blue sweater, caught by the camera mid-leap, one arm flung high above his head, one knee bent up, and a broad smile on his face. We were companionable too, at least as long as we stayed busy. He was as little given to introspection as I was, which made him a highly suitable partner for someone who was not only in denial of great loss but also hiding the lesbian affairs of the past few years. We laughed, ate good meals, went out with his friends, and played a lot of cribbage.

Nothing remains in my memory of a proposal. Probably there wasn't one—or at least not a formal, ring-bearing, down-on-one-knee scene. Maybe it was just assumed. It would have been his style to throw out casually, "When we get hitched, we could pop off to France for a bit," and expect me to digest it without his having to make a fuss. What I do remember, after we announced our engagement, is various family members on both sides telling Colin that he'd have to get a proper job. We should buy a house, they said. Get serious. And, even though I must have sensed we'd never be like the married couples we knew, I entered into these discussions with enthusiasm, hardly noticing if Colin seemed reluctant to leave the river and put on a business suit.

Before we knew it, we had a future: in a few months he would join me in the family ventilation business that my brother had inherited, and where I had gone to work after my three years in Spain and a short stint in public relations. In addition to designing and manu-facturing industrial venting systems, the business now had a thriv-ing domestic department, which I had created, marketing kitchen fans and cooker hoods. In 1968 Britain's gas companies had begun to use the newly abundant North Sea gas, requiring appliances to be adapted and ventilation to be installed in windows all over the country. We acquired a team of glaziers and a fleet of minivans that my brother proposed Colin should manage in the field. Nobody mentioned that since I was a director of the company, his paychecks would bear my signature.

By this time, I was in the habit of going along when he visited his mother on Sunday evenings. Her cottage was right out of an English greeting card, set amid apple trees under which masses of daffodils—mostly white Beershebas—bloomed in spring. But when she emerged to greet me on my first visit, she did not have twinkly eyes or an apron tied around her waist. I remember how uncomfortably I loomed above her in my best coat, hoping for a reversal in our statures so that she might look down on me benignly. I all but bobbed a curtsey while she stood erect in a navy skirt as if on the parade ground. Inside, while Colin was hanging my coat on a peg in the hallway, I caught her looking me up and down. When our eyes met, she smiled brightly and bustled off into the kitchen, leaving me to wonder if I'd passed muster.

Her questions about my family were peremptory and seemed designed only to explore my suitability as an addition to her clan. Colin's sister had married a member of a family whose surname I recognized from Shakespeare plays, and who came attached to a thirteenth-century castle that I would later visit over one exceedingly cold weekend, most of it spent avoiding "the public" who were occasionally let in to look at the gardens. The husband turned out to be a lanky, endearing man who wandered around in baggy corduroy trousers with a shotgun over his shoulder. But I didn't know that yet. All I knew was that Colin's mother was terrifically pleased with her daughter's catch, and much less pleased with Colin's, although she did make some effort to hide it. Over a series of Sunday suppers, she managed to engineer our only connection, a kind of mother-in-law/daughter-in-law alliance, aimed at convincing Colin that he would enjoy the rat race.

BEFORE WE'D set a date, I got pregnant. First I threw up every morning, and then I put on weight. Furtively I had a pregnancy test: negative. I sighed with relief; the thought of having a child filled me with trepidation. By the time I had the second test I was more than four months along and, according to snapshots, showing it.

Only recently legalized, there was still a stigma attached to abortion and many hoops to jump through, but I didn't hesitate. I told no one except Colin, who, I suppose, told Roddy, but neither of them was any use at finding help. So I went to Dr. Brennan, the Scotsman who had been our family doctor as well as my father's weekend fishing friend. After making clear his disapproval, *och aye*-ing and scribbling notes without looking up from his desk, he referred me to someone who referred me to someone else. The final obstacle was a balding, bewildered-looking psychiatrist who made me sit in acute embarrassment for fifty expensive minutes at the end of which he vouched for my imminent insanity.

The private clinic in Hove, whose address he'd jotted on an embossed notepad, smelled of antiseptic and furniture polish. As I stepped into the dark-paneled front hall, the door clicked discreetly shut behind me, and fear fingered the back of my neck. What if it all went wrong?

Sometime after the operation I woke to wave after wave of severe contractions.

"Don't make so much noise," hissed the nurse, glaring at me as I groaned and moaned, thinking I might die. From the moment I'd rung the front doorbell and she had admitted me with a tight smile, she'd made no effort to hide her impatience with my predicament—and now my inability to keep quiet.

"We've sent for the doctor," said the kinder night nurse an hour later and indeed the doctor did make a brief appearance to prescribe a painkiller.

The next day, Colin showed up, carrying a bunch of wildflowers picked from the meadow by his house, a fistful of lavender-blue scabious with one scarlet pimpernel peeping from inside the bunch.

"Hello, Woo," he said, looking uncomfortable on the straight-backed chair beside the bed. "Are you all right then?"

"It was pretty awful." I hesitated while he fidgeted on the chair. "I'm glad you're here."

"Roddy sends his love." Then he fell silent.

Ten minutes later, he announced he was going to a party. I was so weighed down by humiliation and drugs that I couldn't muster any indignation, though I felt sorely abandoned after he left, and remained resentful and sulky for several weeks, which he seemed not to notice. And when was it, I wonder now, that he wrote that poem—the only poem I ever knew him to write, scribbled in pencil on a piece of lined paper that I found years later in some pocket or old handbag, in which he accused me of killing our child? He had never objected to the abortion; could he, all the time, have been harboring fantasies about the son he would have played cricket with and taught to ride? Or did his indignation rise up later when he was already angry at me for my failures as a wife?

Even though I'd never wanted it, I was surprised at how much I thought about the child we might have had. For months I wondered about names, and for several years noted the passing of possible birthdays. It was an odd kind of absence, perhaps more hormonal than anything else. But Colin and I never talked about it. By the time we got married, it was relegated to a growing heap of unapproachable subjects.

ALL SAINTS in Patcham, on the outskirts of Brighton, is a small church with a square Norman tower, surrounded by old oak trees that cast a pleasant shade in summer and an ominous dark in winter. My mother went to the Sunday morning service a few times a year; my father just showed up on Christmas day. They weren't buried there in that traditional English churchyard where the gravestones are mottled with lichen and some lean crookedly away from their neighbors, disturbing the symmetry of the rows; their bodies were taken from the sea to the sprawling cemetery in Gibraltar. But my siblings and I did hold their memorial service at All Saints, the pews filled to overflowing and the Rev. Garston-Smith leaning from the pulpit to speak urgently of my parents. And it was there, seven years later, that the Rev. Garston-Smith married Colin and me.

Wide, flowered hats bumped brims as women kissed cheeks while ushers and a few male guests in morning coats tucked their top hats under their arms as they entered the church and everyone else paraded their frills and furbelows as befitted a showy June wedding. Colin's niece tiptoed behind me in a pink dress with flowers in her hair. The nephew wandered haphazardly in his velvet knickerbockers. I was in white with three arum lilies in my hands and four large brandies under my belt.

The organ blared out the fanfare from Handel's Water Music, its echoes rolling around the blackened roof beams and across the old frescoes on the plaster of the front wall, as I entered on my brother's arm. I walked in my long dress towards the flushed neck and broad shoulders of my future husband. As if in a dream I said "I will" and "till death us do part." I smiled and went *kiss kiss* when the vicar told Colin he could kiss the bride and the bride turned out to be, rather astonishingly, me. After signing the registry, Colin's mother reached up to take my tall brother's arm, and we processed down the aisle, bride and groom, attendant bridesmaids and family, to the triumphant clamor of the Toccata in F by Bach, which I had chosen perhaps for its echoes of Nicolette, or perhaps because I wanted to inject a bit of drama into the day. If there was no grand passion between us, mightn't a piece of music that recalled a grand passion liven up the proceedings?

As I walked towards the door holding onto Colin's arm, the organ was so loud I feared it might blast the old church into pieces. I imagined the fragments flying up into the sky and twirling around before falling in slow motion onto the roofs of nearby houses. The toccata swelled, its chords holding me in their suffocating embrace while the fast-flowing bass notes raced up and down like the soundtrack to a prison escape. Faces on each side of the aisle turned towards us with wedding-day smiles—smiles that for a moment erased their own disappointments, their own failures, their own late-night shouting matches.

Nicolette had demanded a seat near the front. "Your uncle, darling, is your dear departed father's closest living relative. It's only right that we should take our proper place." And there they were, Guy with his mustache waxed at the tips and imposing in an old-fashioned morning suit that smelled faintly of mothballs. Nico seemed to have grown several inches, her head crowned with a many-layered navy turban. She reached out a gloved hand to touch my arm as we passed, a tear glistening in one eye. A few rows back, I glimpsed the beaming face of Jean, and then the red hair of Vivienne, the German teacher with whom I'd had a panicky affair, just weeks before the wedding. On a mission to extend our North Sea gas business into Germany, I'd taken private language classes in the hopes of having a meeting with the men in Dusseldorf, but discovering that I had no aptitude for German, I had taken my teacher along as interpreter. What with the drive across Germany and the turreted castle in which the gas guys put us up, one thing had led to another.

Outside on the grass, we grouped and re-grouped for the photographs, while a blustery wind knocked my lacquered, backcombed hair to one side, and goose bumps ran up and down my arms. At the reception, Nicolette managed to stay sober until close to the end. We barely talked, but she seemed pleased that I was doing the right thing, that I had apparently accepted her version of our affair, which she had once defined as a sort of "trial run." In Italy, she had told me, men were very tolerant of their future wives having premarital sex with other women; in fact, they considered it a useful kind of initiation.

After the bells pealed, the confetti was scattered, glasses raised, and speeches made, I sank into the passenger seat of my white MGB behind the lipstick messages scrawled across the windscreen. As a husband, Colin now became the driver and, dragging a train of clashing tin cans, whisked me away into the dead air of my new closet. Still, I was relieved to have a life without secrets—at least not current ones. Marriage was a pretty good hiding place for a lesbian.

Late that night we arrived in Dieppe where we stayed in a pokey hotel; thousands of motor scooters buzzed past at five in the morning. We went on to Paris, where I took snapshots in the gardens at Versailles—Colin in a pair of zany red pants—and then to the southwest coast near Biarritz. It was a countryside of pine forests, sand dunes, and rabbit stews, with few visitors around. Although I'm sure I told myself that I was happy, the only emotion I can recall is a kind of uneasiness. The perpetual sighing of surf and wind and the murmur of passing travelers' voices were muffled as if at a great distance, while we became a couple of actors playing the honeymoon scene. We ordered local gourmet casseroles, drank a lot of wine, and had sex in hotel beds or on the beach, although I quickly began finding excuses to avoid it.

My skin reddened in the sun and I wrote a lot of postcards, mostly to remind myself of who I used to be before this turn of events, and to pledge that I would soon return to a life I recognized. It was a relief when the white cliffs loomed up and the car ferry disgorged us on to the Newhaven dock. A few hours later, we telephoned our friends and families with glowing reports. Our voices, loud with enthusiasm, must have revealed to any perceptive listener that something was already wrong but if they worried for us, nobody said so.

COLIN'S AND my life soon settled into a predictable routine of work, to which we each drove separately, and weekends with Colin's friends. We often spent evenings at the pub with Roddy, or with the couple who had been Colin's partners in Springs' Smoked Salmon. After a short spell in a depressing, rented flat, we bought a terraced, pink-brick house in Dorking with honeysuckle climbing beside the front steps. I joined the local tennis club, hoping to get to know some of our new neighbors, but many of the women I gravitated to at the club were, it turned out, unhappy in their marriages and I wasn't able to enter into their gripe sessions since I hadn't yet acknowledged, even to myself, that mine wasn't working.

I tried, not very successfully, to cook. We both made the same drive to work, but Colin left a half hour before me, having bathed, shaved, and eaten the eggs, bacon and toast I made for him. My job was at least as demanding as his, but we both took for granted that I would take care of the house and him, in addition to working a full day. He felt free to stop off at the pub on his way home, meet friends, or browse the antique stores where he liked to make deals on Staffordshire figures or lusterware jugs. If he was late for the dinner I had waiting, I rarely complained. But inside I began to fume. Not only was I lonely, I was growing increasingly angry, though I had no idea why: didn't I have an enviable life? Soon, without realizing it, I was simply waiting for an excuse to leave.

One Saturday morning, eleven months after the wedding, Colin shouted out that I should cook his breakfast. Lying in the bathtub, as I often did on weekend mornings, behind a locked door with a good book, my bottled-up resentment spilled out. I surprised myself by yelling, "Get it yourself!" There was a short silence and then a noisy assault on the door, which caved in immediately. Naked, I cringed, feeling, for the first time in my life, physically afraid of someone I knew. He slapped me once on my back and loomed over me for a few minutes, alternately muttering about my laziness and shouting about my duties as a wife. As he stormed down the stairs, I could feel a place on my shoulder blade where the imprint of his hand was reddening my wet skin. I knew I wasn't really hurt except in some internal place that involved pride and my mother's voice telling me to stand up straight because I was beautiful. I pictured the outline of Colin's hand slowly coming into focus like a photograph in a tray of developing liquid and was only distantly aware of the front door slamming.

After a few days of tense standoff and no apologies on either side, I impulsively made plans to take a holiday by myself and told Colin I was going away "to think things over." I flew out to stay with an old school friend who was living with her husband in Barbados where, for a week, I sprawled on the white beach, drank too much rum on the sailing club verandah, and refused to think about my marriage.

In the shade of a Dubonnet-lettered umbrella, I pulled a postcard from the pile waiting next to my glass that now held only a slice of rum-soaked pineapple and scribbled something to Colin. Looking around for the waiter, I glanced across the raked sand to the green-tiled bar in the shade of the palm trees. A lone woman wearing tailored shorts, a bikini top, and a long gauzy scarf wound around her neck perched on one of the high stools. She was leaning in towards the barman in his maroon coat while he shook her cocktail, his arm beckoning and unbeckoning, the ice *thunk-thunking*, his closely cropped head tilting towards her with a hint of intimacy. Then she turned away from him and stared directly at me. When the breeze kicked up a sand devil at her feet and the two tails of her emerald scarf floated into the air, for a brief moment I thought it was Nicolette.

STEPPING OFF the 727 at Gatwick and staggering up the tunnel into the airport, I had a bad headache. There, in the crush of family re-unions and embracing couples, stood Colin, a bunch of roses in his hand. He kissed me on the cheek and thrust the flowers at me.

"There you are, Woo," he said. "I missed you."

Driving round the ring road in stop-and-go traffic, he asked me nothing about my trip. My sunburn itched and my whole being re-belled against the smell of diesel; I wanted to be back with the scents of oleander, the sounds of steel bands, crashing surf, and ice cubes clinking in a frosty glass. I listened half-heartedly while he filled me in on things at work and the score of his weekend cricket match, but I was overcome by a kind of weariness, a lassitude against which there was no point rallying. It was all over, and I knew it. But why? How could I explain? I'd gone away to think but I had no idea how to con-duct an inner life. I glanced sideways at his profile, remembering the fondness I had once felt for his crooked nose and the ginger sideburns that curled when they grew too long.

Back at our house we sat down at the kitchen table with bread and butter, a plate of cold ham, and a limp lettuce. Between us, the roses in a cut glass vase began to open, their heavy fragrance crowding into the room. I could hardly breathe. Hadn't I married him because he was nicer than the others? Couldn't we start again?

Colin leaned towards me hesitantly. "Listen," he said, his voice shaky. "I understand the problem now. I know what's wrong and I think we can get through it."

Dread turned the pit of my stomach. I didn't know what I was afraid of, but I was definitely afraid.

"What do you mean?" Whatever he was going to say, it involved my wrongness, of that I was sure.

"I found your letters."

I stared at him.

Then, "What letters?"

"The letters in your suitcase."

I knew which suitcase he meant. It was a white leather one. Full of Nicolette's letters, and some of Jean's.

"That suitcase is locked."

"Well, I broke the lock," he said. "I knew you had something to hide and now I know what it is. You can change."

He looked first defiant and then, when he remembered, awkwardly concerned. Soon he was merely flustered: there were too many things he knew but couldn't bring himself to say.

"You broke into my suitcase?" I said, beginning to feel rage welling up.

"Well, I had to . . ."

"What do you mean, 'had to'?" Now I was getting hot.

"Don't shout at me. Anyway, Joan said . . ."

"What do you mean 'Joan said'? Are you talking about my *godmother*?" I was losing my balance.

"When she saw Nicolette's letters, she said that woman always causes trouble and she wasn't surprised she had led you into this . . ."

"I'm leaving you," I said, cool again. I felt dead inside.

This time it was Colin's turn to say, "What do you mean?," but I could only say dully, "It's over."

"Well," he said, his voice shaking and his eyes fearful, "if you leave me, I'll stand up in court and tell everybody everything. The whole damned world will know you're a lesbian!"

This was the second time that word had hung in the air between me and an antagonist. It was just as potent now as it had been in the car, parked on Birdcage Walk, when I'd hurled it at Nicolette. Its three hated syllables slapped my face, making me recoil with a jerk of my neck; my knees began to tremble.

Nothing in the world could be worse than having my dirty secret revealed but, scared as I was, I knew I couldn't stay. My life was probably over anyway.

"Do what you want," I said and went upstairs to pack.

THREE DECADES after the divorce, I was curious about Colin and wrote him a letter: maybe I could drop in the next time I was in England? Colin's response was cautious. But he did offer a cup of tea and directions to his house.

It was one of those mild, rosy-brick kind of English days with no wind and gentle sunshine when I knocked at the door. Colin appeared round the side of the house from the garden, where he'd been setting out the cups and saucers on a picnic table. I never did go inside, but waited on the lawn, observing his neatly staked dahlias and an abundance of scarlet runner beans, until he returned with the teapot in its knitted cozy and a plate of biscuits. I remembered that cozy—it had been his mother's, but when I volunteered this, he told me that she had recently died.

"Oh, I'm so sorry," I said, meaning it.

Colin seized the teapot and poured the industrial strength tea he had always favored into the chipped china cups, while I took a good look at him.

He seemed very much the same with just a hint of gray in his dark hair, and as we talked, I realized that his looks were not the only thing that remained unchanged. His life still consisted of work, riding, cricket, and football. Roddy, who had married the girlfriend I knew in the old days, often stopped by for dinner, or had him over to the house in Henfield. Colin hadn't remarried.

He told me about a girlfriend he'd had for a while, a nurse from whom he claimed to have learned a lot about women. He meant sex, although he didn't say the word, but he did give me a kind of rueful glance.

I looked away, took a chocolate digestive biscuit, and changed the subject. A squirrel ran up the trellis that divided the garden from his neighbors'.

"Do you still have Frank?" I asked, and then realized that Frank would be awfully old by now, and that Colin, his mother recently dead, might not want to talk about his very old or dead horse.

"Why?" he demanded, suddenly angry. "You want me to cut him in half so you can get your share?"

Colin had been bitter when we'd agreed, through our lawyers, to sell the house and share the proceeds; this wasn't the first time he'd suggested that I wanted to chop up Frank. He'd never been able to get his head around no-fault divorce, and apparently still couldn't, remaining resentful that I'd been entitled to half our assets. His logic was, if I chose to leave him, why shouldn't I pay through the nose? Back then, I'd been equally combative, reminding him that he'd ended up working with my brother and earning a good salary, whereas I had felt obliged to disappear.

Ignoring his outburst, I admired the vegetables in their well-mulched beds. The English sunshine was so calm; the air so still. Yet, everything I'd gone through since I left it behind had been not calm, not still, nothing like this polite teatime ritual. I felt as if I'd slipped back in time for a moment into a past which was fiercely familiar, yet didn't fit—it never had, not even then.

I observed Colin's tastefully ragged clothes which, as always, sat nicely on his hips. I remembered the overnight trips from which he used to return with pottery for his collection, and the mysterious antique dealers who had called our house so regularly. Then I wondered, as I had so many times before, whether he, too, had all along been nursing a secret self. He looked up and smiled apologetically. He would have made the sweetest gay man.

IMAGINE

THE 1970s were breaking open when I landed at my friend Lydia's flat in St John's Wood. She and her flatmate were wearing black and hanging out in the local pub with a group of artists and writers. I was impressed by their casual mention of the publishers or galleries that might at any time discover them. I leaned against the bar, jutting out my hip in what I hoped was a cool fashion and once went home with a drunk playwright, who recited the whole first act of his masterpiece before he passed out on the sofa. Most nights, after the pub closed, we went on to parties where beer coated the linoleum and invariably someone threw up.

It hadn't even been a full year since I had summoned friends and family to the white lace and champagne all around, then, without explanation, made an abrupt exit from my marriage with Colin. Now I was making nobody's breakfast but my own. Weaving through the traffic around Hyde Park Corner, I headed to work in Mitcham passing through those southern reaches of London that were littered with vinegar-stained newspapers. The grass on Clapham Common was muddy and its dogs dispirited, but inside my purple Mini, the space was mine and mine alone; my energy filled it up and pressed outward against the windows as I sang along with John Lennon's "Imagine." I burned rubber on the corners, floored the accelerator, and hurled the little car into every straight as if it were an extension of my own body sprinting towards the unknown. I didn't know what kind of world I wanted to dream up, but I felt delirious listening to John's version.

It was Lydia who provided the clue. Before she disappeared to visit her parents one Sunday, she left *The Times* strewn across her brown velvet couch, the color magazine damp from the bathroom. The clock plodded along as I read the paper with less than half my mind, picking up and throwing down sections. Then the headline "Women's Liberation Workshop" caught my eye—just a brief paragraph about a new location where reading materials and information about women's groups could be found.

I'd never paid much attention to politics. My first date had taken me to the Young Conservatives Ball, which I didn't think of as connected to a political party: it was merely where young men and women like me dressed up to go and foxtrot once a year. Over time I'd fallen away from the assumptions of my Tory family, though I'd failed to develop an alternative point of view. Now, having walked out of an eleven-month marriage and with the age of thirty threatening to land in a couple of years, I felt restless; the sound of "Women's Liberation Workshop" whispered like a titillating proposition in my ear as I plodded through another work week.

Oxford Street was deserted the following Sunday when I cruised along with the *Times* clipping on the passenger seat. I glanced at it to check the name of the street off Piccadilly Circus. Approaching the statue of Eros, his wings spread above the splashing fountain, his one leg lifted in a joyful dance, I thought about turning round and going back to Lydia's. But I didn't. I went on, peering up at the street signs.

Shavers Place turned out to be a narrow alley. I parked at the end and walked past dumpsters and unmarked doors. When I found the right one and pushed it open, a sign, hand-drawn with a black felt pen, declared: "Women's Liberation: upstairs." In case the staircase itself was not clear enough, a wobbly arrow pointed the way. The cramped room

I stepped into was covered on three walls with metal bookshelves; in front of a sooty window, a desk held several rolodexes and stacks of a mimeographed newsletter. A woman in jeans and a flannel shirt, laundered to a faint memory of its Black Watch tartan, swiveled to face the room. Three others sat on the floor, chatting and drinking Nescafé. A half pint milk bottle occupied the one empty chair.

The woman at the desk probably thought I'd come to the wrong place; I was suddenly aware of the careful creases in my petrol blue trouser suit.

"Yeah?" she said.

"Sorry," I said, unprepared to explain myself. "I just thought maybe I'd pick up some . . ." I shrugged apologetically.

Softening a bit, the woman handed me a newsletter and flashed a quick smile that revealed a front tooth twisted sideways. I smiled back, but she clamped her lips down as if too much had been revealed and gestured with her head to the shelves, where piles of stapled papers were stacked.

The three women on the floor scooted closer together, stirring up dust. Murmuring "sorry" again, I walked carefully round them.

"Lists are free," the desk woman said to my back, "and the articles are marked."

I thanked her and wandered about, picking up papers randomly while she sorted the newsletters into piles; the others stopped talking and I could feel them watching me. Flustered, I threw some money into the donation box and hurried down the stairs. Just before I opened the street door, I heard a burst of laughter from above. Were they laughing at me?

Back at the flat, I made myself a mug of tea and sat down to examine my haul. The first title was printed in bold capitals: "The Myth of the Vaginal Orgasm." I quickly put it face down on the couch beside me, though there was no one home to catch me reading it. I'd heard the word "vaginal" used in a medical context, but nobody had ever said the O-word in my presence: I'd become familiar with the thing itself during sex with women, though never in my marriage. Now, picking it up and reading on, I discovered that not only could one say it and think about it, one could write a treatise on the subject, which apparently had been neglected in "the male literature." Strange, I'd never thought of literature as male or female before. Reading my way through the pile of papers, I discovered that housework bloody well ought to be paid for, that women's clothes symbolize our oppression, and that if we told the truth about our lives the world would split open.

At the bottom of the stack I came across a single sheet headed "Consciousness Raising Groups: London." I had no idea what such a group did, but I scanned the list for my part of town as if it were exactly what I'd been looking for. When I phoned the Holland Park group, I reached Lilian.

"Yup?" she answered in a nonchalant American accent. I mumbled something about the group and she told me the next meeting was on Wednesday at someone's flat. I wrote down the address.

On Monday morning, driving to work past the houseboats moored along Chelsea Reach, I wondered if I would go to the meeting and if I did, what it would be like. I continued to think about it as I sat at my desk pushing paperwork around until my brother and I, as usual, crossed the road for lunch at the pub. We rushed through our steak and kidney pie and downed a half of bitter, but when he asked how I'd spent my weekend, I changed the subject. The upcoming meeting was beginning to feel like a secret, even before I'd decided to go.

AS I rang the bell, I felt sweat on my forehead; would they see through the reticence with which I usually managed to disguise my ignorance? I was ushered upstairs to a room where six women were sitting in a circle, some on the floor. The light bulbs were dim and the lamp in the corner didn't reveal much of the recently vacuumed rug or old furniture that someone had sanded into lightness. The posters on the wall were not political ones but Picassos and Matisses. A couple of the women nodded at me; two studied me with overt curiosity, and one offered a cup of tea. I sipped the strong brew from a mug with a picture of Freud on it until the last two members arrived. Lilian then took charge, though I later learned that no one was supposed to be the leader.

"Well, here we are again," she said, by way of starting the meeting. It would be months before I realized that jaded was her primary public persona: to be jaded implied long experience with radical politics, disappointment with her fellow feminists, and a kind of weariness that went with having been there from the beginning.

Then she brightened up. "And we have a newcomer," she said.

When everyone turned to me, I realized I was supposed to speak. Blushing, I said, "My name's Judy . . . umm . . . I found out about this group at the office." They were still looking at me but I couldn't think of a single thing to add.

Fortunately, Lilian charged ahead and I sank back into my chair. "Before we get to tonight's topic, let's all agree to go to the next collective meeting, shall we? Shavers Place, as usual, is in fucking disarray."

I recognized the street name, though I'd never come across a collective and, moreover, had never heard anyone use the word fuck before. The casual way it slipped into Lilian's sentence was shocking, though soon I, too, would find it indispensable to opinionated speech. I looked at her more closely. She lounged in an overstuffed armchair, with one leg crooked over its arm. Her face, beginning to show lines, revealed that she was older than I had supposed at first. As I watched, she shifted in the chair to sit upright, crossing her legs and tucking her bare feet under her thighs; she must have done more than a few years of yoga.

My ears registered a variety of accents, two American, one north country, and the rest London—all some version of middle class. Lilian was the most casually dressed in tight jeans; one of the others looked as if she'd come straight from her job in a jacket and skirt, and everyone else, including me, wore slacks. There was no sign of makeup and I was glad I'd kept mine to a minimum and left my hair to frizz out of its carefully straightened bob. The woman who had let me in appeared the most studious with her wire-rimmed glasses and dark hair that fell over her face. She referred, several times, to books she had read, her slight stammer growing more pronounced with excitement, and once she scuttled over to a bookshelf made of bricks and planks to pull out a volume by Doris Lessing.

The topic of that evening was "femininity." I tried to listen to the women talking, while at the same time thinking of what to say. I was toying with telling them about Victor Sylvester's dance school, where, at fifteen, I had been sent to acquire some necessary graces. Perfumed, middle-aged women had waltzed in each other's arms while terrified young men in ties and shiny shoes hovered behind pillars. We few teenage girls sat on the gold-painted, mock-Regency chairs in a line near the lemonade table, our hands folded in our laps to hold down the layers of net petticoats that threatened to spring up, lifting our skirts out in front of us to reveal a knee or a thigh or a wayward garter. At the grand piano, our pianist lifted her hands dramatically in the air and turned towards us, her penciled eyebrows raised and an encouraging smile on her powdered face, while the man in the blue suit cued us up for a quickstep. She nodded meaningfully towards the boys and thumped out opening chords. Slowly, they emerged, hands in pockets, trying to look as if they didn't care which girl they ended up in front of. Those of us still sitting by the middle of the dance would get up as if lemonade was what we'd wanted all along, and mutter to each other about how the boys got stupider and uglier each week.

For me, there wasn't much to choose between getting picked, which would mean looming over a boy who hadn't noticed my six-foot height until I stood up, or joining the gang of the spurned. The only part I didn't mind was learning the dance steps when we spread out around the ballroom partnerless. Standing carefully on the footprints painted on the floor I would wobble as my femininity wavered and my low-heeled white shoes stuck their pointed toes out beyond the snub-toed diagrams.

"Step right foot forward," the instructor said with exaggerated patience, "Now, ladies turn to face the window. Gentlemen slide to your right and face the fire door." We lumbered around, some clockwise, others counterclockwise, then searched the floor for another footprint. Hovering on one foot, I desperately scanned the polished floorboards for a resting place, like some ungainly bird coming in to land.

But I wasn't sure if this was the kind of story they'd want to hear.

For weeks I watched and listened, smiling or nodding. While I remained reticent, the others spilled their outrage. "Why the fuck am I supposed to wash up and clean the loo and pick up his socks, even though I have a job too?" someone might burst out, and the rest of us would murmur our solidarity. The two Americans, who had not been raised to believe complaining was a cardinal sin, were much less inhibited than the others; admiring their matter-of-fact revelations, I managed to speak up more each week as we discussed our bodies, our abortions, and whether it was right to shave our legs.

I'd never had the intimate talks that bind best friends together, having always been cautious about revealing my secrets, nor had I particularly missed them, but now I started to long for an intimate friend with whom I could reveal myself and be seen. Hell, I wanted to see my own self! Week after week, we took long breaths and with our hearts beating in our ears, we translated our lives into rambling narratives. We were learning how to listen to one another in a new way—a way that encouraged us to understand things we'd rarely thought and never heard said aloud.

Those meetings—now half a century ago—have merged into one long piece of music, sometimes moving along repetitively like a Philip Glass symphony with many different melodies merging into one another, and occasionally erupting into a storm of percussion like Verdi's *Dies Irae* crashing through the room. Someone would run to the door sobbing and, for the next few days, the rest of us would take turns calling her, urging her to try again, and usually, after a week or two, she'd show up.

Although I was growing accustomed to our frank talks, when the group decided that the next-but-one discussion would focus on lesbianism, I almost fainted. I'd read enough of the pamphlets from Shavers Place to know that it wouldn't be considered awful here, but nevertheless I was terrified that the truth about me would destroy my fragile connection to these women.

As I went about my days, a blurry image of the two teenage girls who had been expelled from my school drifted across the back of my mind. Although they hadn't been in my form, when someone told me they'd been thrown out I had known immediately who they were. One was big, a solid presence with wide brown eyes; the other has dissolved except as part of the inseparable couple—the two who walked hand in hand and sometimes lay in the long grass around the edge of the lacrosse field, hands touching in the jungle of clover, perhaps even holding each other face to face when they thought no one was around.

Many of us at school had been preoccupied with amours that sometimes became the subject of teasing but were fundamentally respectable. The object of our desire was called a "pash" and mine was Mary Howell-Davis, the captain of the first lacrosse team—as tough and muscular a girl as that position demanded. In spite of the fact that I hated lacrosse, I went out on the worst days to watch Mary tearing the length of the field, twisting past defenders with the ball tucked securely into her stick, which she cradled in time with her thudding feet and held dangerously close to her face. It was not unusual for good lacrosse players to get their teeth knocked out, but my heroine was immune, so swiftly did she run on her shapely legs, so deftly did she duck and weave through the defense line. For a year, I wrote her initials all over my notebook, sometimes twined into a heart . . . but that wasn't what the meeting was going to be about.

Night after night, I rehearsed. Standing in front of the bathroom mirror, I attempted to say "I am a lesbian," but I couldn't, not even alone. I struck an offhand pose with one hand on my hip and drawled the words; I sprawled in an armchair and threw out the words with a chuckle. Desperately, I tried being theoretical: "My own experience shows that it's not acceptable in this society to relate sexually to women." That was easier though it was a cop-out; they probably wouldn't even catch the confession buried inside "my own experience."

When the meeting finally arrived, I didn't know what would come out of my mouth. I felt distinctly nauseous as Rosemary, sitting next to me, began speaking confidently. "I'm open to it," she said. The others sat up straighter and looked at her with new interest.

One by one, they declared their support for "women-identified women," interrupted only by periodic searches for coins to keep the gas fire going. When it was Lilian's turn, she claimed that many of the leaders of the first wave of feminism had been lesbians. That fact, of course, had been written out of history, she said, but we could and would write it back in. All my new companions were, I realized, quite unafraid of the topic: they might just as well have been talking about whalebone corsets for all the effect it had on them. I, however, was becoming a wreck.

The hope for an honest life that had always prowled outside in the night like a coyote—its yellow eyes reminding me of some beautiful, terrifying possibility—had now moved into broad daylight. If I fed it, maybe it would stick around.

"Your turn, Judy," someone said, and faces turned towards me. I could feel the coyote's warm breath on my neck.

"Well," I said, hating the color that threatened to swamp my face. "Well . . . actually . . . umm . . . I've slept with several women."

The group not only perked up, they positively levitated. When I sank back into my chair, they realized I wasn't about to elaborate, at least not yet.

LILIAN ACQUIRED pamphlets from New York well before they appeared at Shavers Place. She was withering about what she labeled middle-of-the-road feminism and keen on the Redstockings, the New York group whose manifesto had declared women an oppressed class and called for an analysis of our common situation. Swept along by her certainty, just a couple of months after reading my first position paper, I'd become a radical feminist.

That November of 1972 our whole group went to the Second National Women's Liberation Conference held at Acton Town Hall. At the plenary session where we were to create policy statements for the UK movement as a whole, the hall grew dense with smoke and argument. Twenty minutes into the meeting, a woman sprinted from the second row on to the stage and grabbed the microphone from the hand of a beleaguered woman who was trying to explain childcare arrangements. I gasped as the intruder began to shout out a series of slogans: this was clearly not going to be an orderly affair. After a while, though, I got used to it as woman after woman ran up to grab the mike and the audience loosened up enough to heckle.

"We'll never get anywhere if we're run by a bunch of fucking separatists," yelled a nimble, catlike woman who had managed to seize her moment on stage. To which Lilian and half a dozen others hurled a chorus of responses.

"We won't get anywhere under the thumb of the fucking male-dominated left either!"

"This is a *women's* movement, assholes!"

As the morning progressed, I realized that we were sitting in clumps of the ideologically like-minded: radical feminists on one side of the room and socialist feminists opposite. Scattered around were a few others I would come to recognize—five or six disheveled Maoists, two rows of respectable equal-pay types, and several journalists whose philosophy was unclear. The divides were sharper and fiercer than I'd realized, although the various camps looked very much the same: six hundred pairs of blue jeans sat on six hundred metal folding chairs. The only skirt in the room belonged to a woman with a cloud of red hair and she could get away with it because she'd been in jail. Anyway, as I saw when she prowled onto the stage and began to speak, it was a denim skirt.

Lilian whispered that the skirt-woman and her lover had been arrested and held in connection with an IRA conspiracy, though everyone knew that the police had planted the evidence and the two had eventually been let go. According to the rumor mill—which often preferred a good story over an accurate one—one of them had a posh mother who visited them in prison and burst into tears at the sight of her daughter. But both the prisoners behaved as if it were perfectly normal for young ladies of their background to entertain the family in Holloway. Since things could hardly get any worse, they seized the moment.

"Listen, mum," announced the daughter, "I might as well tell you now. I'm a lesbian."

"That's nice darling," sniffed her mother, mopping her eyes and smiling vaguely towards the lover, who was loitering nearby.

Now, as her eloquence rolled over the crowd, the vowels, as well as the skirt, revealed that she was one of the few non-American leaders. Her fingers were long and sexy. Her calves—the only ones visible the whole weekend—were firm and revolutionary. She quoted Marx frighteningly often and each time she did, her skirt whipped against her legs as she whirled around looking for detractors. She was utterly terrifying.

Lilian, however, dismissed all this Marxism as irrelevant. We were separatists, she said, her cornflower blue eyes deceptively sweet. All that male theory was for the boys: we weren't going to bother with it anymore. The other members of our group looked relieved; their mothers didn't want communist daughters either. As for me, I was relieved because I hadn't read Marx and didn't want anyone to find out.

When the session ended, there was a scraping of chairs and a burst of excited chatter as women wandered into the hallways to examine an array of smudgy position papers. At one table sat a young woman who looked familiar. I examined the books, eyeing her cautiously until suddenly it hit me: St Mary's Hall!

"Sometimes you took us for prep," the young woman said, laughing, but I could think of nothing at all to say, so shocking was it to discover that someone from my old school had found her way here too.

I was threading a path through the throngs and heading for the door, ready to slip off and have a sandwich, when I noticed a group of women sitting on a bench. One was wearing black jeans, something that I'd never seen before. Two had leather jackets. And two were kissing. Not a darling-how-lovely-to-see-you kiss on the cheek. And not a see-you-later-dear peck either. A real, low-down, tongues-involved, smooch. I stood stock still, staring until one of the two who were kissing—the one looking in my direction—caught my eye. Her mouth being otherwise occupied, she couldn't smile, although the top of her face around the eyes did that thing that faces do when there's a grin about. I was nowhere near ready to smile back.

At the dance that evening the six hundred pairs of jeans gyrated, stretched, and bopped across the wooden floor to a women's rock band. Beer splashed from paper cups and smoke piled up so thick you could barely see the door if you happened to be watching for someone. (I was trying not to watch too obviously for the black jeans or the leather jackets.) Most women danced in groups or alone, weaving through the crowd, hooking up with another dancer for a few minutes, and then melting away. In the corner, I thought I saw two couples holding each other, dancing close. I threw myself vigorously into our group effort. Lilian, who deplored the uptight dancing of the British, squatted low and tossed her long hair backwards and forwards.

Collapsing onto a rickety wooden chair by the wall, I lit a cigarette and watched women flinging off their flannel shirts and letting their bare breasts bounce. I felt strangely peaceful, as if I'd always known that one day I'd end up here.

"*Hal*-lo der." The faintly foreign vowels belonged to a stately woman with fine blonde hair that fell below her waist, and a soggy, hand-rolled cigarette stuck to her lip.

I stood and gave her the chair so she could prop up her leg, which was in a plaster cast to the knee. She turned out to be Monica Sjoo, a Swedish painter who was notorious since the women's art exhibition at the Swiss Cottage Library had been closed down by the police on account of her six-foot tall painting: "God Giving Birth." Soon she would come to fascinate, inspire, and very briefly seduce me, but for now I tried not to appear too interested.

There was a stir at the door. Dancers started moving towards the table where we'd paid to get in. Monica beckoned to someone who had left the crowd and was strolling past us.

"What's up?"

The woman shrugged. "It's just some blokes in drag trying to get in." She looked impressively bored and wandered on.

"Faggots!" said Monica, heaving herself out of the chair, "Bloody men think they belong everywhere!"

As the rumor of an invasion of men scurried around the floor, more and more women stopped dancing and turned to watch the entrance. A few pulled on their discarded shirts, leaving them unbuttoned while they waited to see what would happen. The band played on, banging out a beat that rattled the beer kegs. The crowd by the door gradually moved back, parting as if to make way for royalty, while at the same time linking arms to create a barrier. Two figures appeared and stood motionless. When one of them raised a commanding hand, the band stopped, the drum petering out in a trickle of thumps.

Excessively tall and slender, the newcomers might have been young women from a Henry James novel. They both wore elaborate gowns that hugged their bodies, buttoned shoes, sweeping hats and elbow-length white gloves. One had dark curls that fell onto the shoulder straps of her pale green dress. The other wore yellow and a hat adorned with narcissi. Slowly, swinging their parasols, they moved forward into the room. Women started to whisper: "Don't let them in, they're men!" but the strangers just strolled on as if they were at a Buckingham Palace garden party. They paraded in a circle, stepping out with pointed toes, swiveling their upper torsos to the left and right. Monica nudged me in the ribs. "I know them," she hissed. "It's Jackie and Pat. I know them."

"Jackie and Pat?" I repeated stupidly, thinking she meant the male versions of those names.

"They're women," Monica said firmly, "This is an *action*."

"Oh, I see," I said, not getting it in the least.

Pretty soon the two interlopers arrived back at the doorway. They turned one last time to face the wall of women and threw out handfuls of business cards. I walked out on to the dance floor and picked one up. "Sistershow," it said. "Feminist political theatre by Jackie Thrupp and Pat Van Twest." When I looked up, they'd already sashayed out the door and a buzz was going around the room. Women were starting to defend their right to dress the way they wanted, no matter that they all adopted the same look. "What the fuck was all that about? Who are they to make fun of us?" someone demanded. We were not yet accustomed to being sent up by our own. "Did you see those shoes?" someone else muttered.

Eventually, the band struck up again. Monica hobbled out on her cast pulling me along, my arm firmly clasped in her large, paint-flecked hand. Lilian boogied around with our group and the crowd began to dance, singing along, soon shouting with the band: "Freedom's just another word for nothin' left to lose . . ."

The room started to pulse; I stripped off my shirt, twirled it high and tossed it away. I stamped my feet to the beat and melted into the rhythm of the crowd. How had I come to belong among these wild, smart women who danced and kissed and, I had no doubt, would surely change the world? I loved their bravado, their bluster, and their astonishing belief in themselves and each other. Even now that female energy remains so seductive that I have to remind myself of the painful hostilities, the recklessness, and the pettiness that existed alongside the bravery.

I STRUGGLED to keep pace with my own rapid changes: my appearance, my allegiances, and most of my beliefs, to say nothing of a whole new set of friends. Trying to make up for years of obliviousness, I questioned everything: how my boss at BBC Television, (a man who barely needed one secretary) had expected me, the junior one, only to look good and feed the goldfish; my father whose word had been law and the ways in which my mother worked around that ("let him think it was his idea"); the absence of women—except for queens and the occasional wife—in the history books I'd read at school. And how could I not have noticed the bruises under the powder layered on the cheekbone of that woman at Tesco who'd argued with the checkout clerk and threatened to give her whining toddler something to cry about?

I was jolted daily, sometimes even hourly, by insights that have since become commonplace, as new ways of understanding the world always do in the end. Trying to make sense of it all, I wrote copiously in notebooks, scrawling quotations from the theorists: Juliet Mitchell, Kate Millet, Eva Figes, and the poets: Alta, Robin Morgan, and Astra. Often, I would pull my car over after a meeting and stop to write down a thought. At night I sat up in bed making notes or woke up before dawn to record a dream. It was as if a door had opened where I'd never even known a door existed; I'd walked through it and entered a landscape that looked familiar at first—but the light was different, the geographical features out of place, and the weather much more unpredictable.

My familiar drive to work had been transformed. Streatham High Street was filled with women who, at any moment, might chuck away their string bags, vegetables scattering hither and thither, and link arms as if they were in a Bollywood movie, with revolution breaking out all around them. Brixton, which had always felt rather foreign, hovering for several years on the verge of race riots, no longer scared me; I recognized the urgency among the stalls of its street market.

Like most new converts to anything, I was extreme. For the moment, sexism explained everything: my father, Colin, all the ex-boyfriends, became part of a male world which had wronged me and all women. While much of the theory would hold up over time and I would remain a committed feminist, I would sooner or later have to grapple with complexities not apparent during those heady first months.

I moved out from Lydia's and sublet a flat in Pimlico where I could live alone. Next to the toilet, I tacked up typewritten copies of my favorite poems, several of which were by Susan Griffin, whose first book we passed from hand to hand, increasingly dog-eared and coffee-ringed. Lilian discovered that I was writing poems and suggested we put together another group, this one for writers. We found seven poets and named ourselves the Literature Collective. Now I had two weekly meetings, a monthly meeting at Shavers Place, and numerous speak-outs, conferences, and events with titles like "Women in History" or "Women and Psychiatry"—all beset by ideological confrontations.

On weekdays, I woke up dreading work. As the marketing director of our family business, I was getting a substantial salary and driving a company-owned car, but certainly not putting in a full day. I began to feel uncomfortable with being a boss, leaving my secretary to run things while I went to meetings or dropped in to help with re-wiring the Shepherd's Bush house we were renovating as a Women's Centre. After too many months of arriving late and leaving early, not to mention having to run into Colin, I decided to quit. My brother was perplexed. He'd given me a secure position; what on earth was I doing? I couldn't explain: my new life felt utterly disconnected from all of them—the before and the after unbridgeable.

Although I'd blown almost all my small inheritance years earlier, I didn't stop to worry about how I would survive. Many of the women I knew were unemployed and on the dole, so I signed on too; then I joined forces with Lilian and a new member of our group, Zelda, who had been talking about setting up an alternative removal service. Most feminists had little spare cash but they did move house frequently, taking with them favorite pieces of furniture or items a parent had passed on to them like a wardrobe or a washing machine. A number of fringe moving companies advertised in *Time Out*, the best known of them optimistically named "Gentle Ghosts"—lefty men who frequently turned out to be sexist, patronizing, or the kiss of death to the piano.

"Could we actually carry a piano?" We looked dubiously at one another. A grin spread across Zelda's face and the three of us roared with laughter. *Of course* we could. We could do anything.

When we looked at the prices of suitable secondhand vehicles, we almost gave up. Then a friend of Zelda's offered an ancient, red Bedford van with dents all over its snub nose and very loose steering. We put down £10 and he agreed we could pay it off over a few months, depending on how well the money came in. We thought perhaps a wider range of services would boost our revenue—after all there were lots of things we could do—so I sold myself as a driving instructor and Lilian offered editing. We debated doing childcare, but Lilian, the only mother among us, was tired of responsibility for children, and neither Zelda nor I felt up to it. We slapped each other on the back when one of us came up with the name, "She Can Do It," and right away composed an advertisement for the next newsletter.

Now my meeting-filled life expanded to include trips in the van, the three of us singing as we rattled into remote regions of London to haul refrigerators, beds, and tea chests up and down stairs. It was a point of honor to accept every job that came along. Doubled over, red-faced, and panting on a half-landing with some heavy object propped against the wall, we chanted, "brains over brawn; brains over brawn."

When the van spluttered and died, we spent hours waiting on street corners for our mechanic friend to show up. This entrepreneurial life was physically demanding and minimally lucrative, but we didn't neglect our politics as we argued with clients and one another, unpacking the implications of each decision.

I squeezed in appointments with the two who signed up for driving lessons. Valerie, a brown-skinned, athletic young woman who lived off Clapham Common, was jittery with nerves and itching to change her mind about driving. She jumped in and out of the car, first taking the passenger seat, while I gave her my talk about safety, and then slipping into the driving seat even while declaring loudly that she'd had enough for the day. As we settled in for a chat, I asked where she came from.

"Born in Brixton," she snapped. And then, after a long pause, "Parents from Pakistan."

"Oh," was the best I could manage. I hadn't had much practice with this sort of conversation. Diversity, in the women's movement of that era in London was all about class, not race.

"Do you know Sally?" I mustered, "She's one of the workers at the workshop. You've probably seen her there. A . . . mmm . . . very young *colored* girl."

"A colored girl?" Valerie snapped louder this time. "A colored girl? We're all colored, hadn't you noticed that?" Then she sighed deeply and went on, "Brown, black, red. . . . You, for instance, are a colored woman, aren't you?" She was poking towards my chest.

"White!" Valerie shouted. "That's your color. White! Get it?"

I was too embarrassed to look at her.

"I'm quite ready now," she said confidently.

My voice was unusually quiet as I talked her through putting the car into first gear and suggested that she very slowly release the clutch. As if breaking from the Derby's starting gate, the Mini took a leap forward, the tires screamed, and we raced down the narrow street straight into a line of dustbins that we hit with great force. Fortunately, shock caused Valerie to release the gas pedal, while I hauled on the parking brake. Garbage, mostly consisting of rotten cabbages, rolled away from us, and we both burst out laughing. It bonded us well enough to guarantee a month's worth of lessons.

My only other client was the husband of my former secretary, who was excellent on the internal mysteries of my Mini's motor, but hard on the clutch. Luckily, neither one of them killed me.

WOMEN IN my group had started dropping by. Bed-hopping, not only in my circle but in the movement at large, had become as common as going to the pub for a pint. They were all eager to try it with a woman.

Rosemary was the first, ringing the bell one night after eleven and looking coy when I opened the door; it wasn't long before she was staying the night once or twice a week, even though she lived with a boyfriend she was disinclined to give up. She concocted stories for him involving late meetings or out of town conferences. Once, she persuaded me to go to Brighton for a weekend where she promised we would walk by the sea and read *Martha Quest* aloud.

It never occurred to me to say no, nor actively to pursue my own choice of a lover; I simply went along with the eager seductions that came my way. Not that I was immune to Rosemary's charms—I wasn't. But the boyfriend situation irritated me and anyway, I preferred to read by myself.

Returning from Brighton, I stopped in Notting Hill at a phone box to call Lilian, having promised to drop in and see her if we got back in time. Rosemary, observing my body language through the car window, understood even before I did that Lilian was about to replace her. She flung open the car door and stomped off down Ladbroke Grove back to the boyfriend.

A few days later, Lilian turned up at noon with homemade soup and a baguette. Perched on the stool in my kitchen, she stirred automatically while she looked at me intently. While it simmered, some powerful connection between us locked into place with an almost audible click. She started spending every day with me and, since her husband and children were still living with her, returning to her house before the kids got home from school. In cold weather, we shopped at the local deli for bread and pâté, heated up canned soup, and had picnics in bed after making love. When the sun shone, we strolled through the neighborhood and stretched out in Hyde Park or in the grounds of the Chelsea Hospital, where we read aloud Judy Grahn's *Edward the Dyke*. I adored poor Edward who was too tall for her evil psychiatrist's couch and who was frequently mistaken for a man when she went into a public loo. Since I'd given up makeup and hair care, this had started happening to me too and I knew it was not simply my height that provoked the mistakes, but some other aspect of how I claimed my space. When it first started, I would blush and feel profoundly wrong. I took to creeping into the ladies' with caution and smiling with an almost-pleading expression. Sometimes I entered humming at a high pitch. Occasionally I had fantasies of ripping open my shirt to display my bare breasts; I wondered if I would ever, like Edward, be able to tell the women who bristled at me that I was "really only a harmless dyke."

I tried not to think about Lilian's husband, who struck me as a very decent guy, though I only met him once or twice before he moved back to the States. He supported her political activities and was willing to do his share of childcare, but it was disconcerting to know that Lilian left me to set the table for a family dinner and, later, to climb up to their bedroom. Perhaps it was just a ploy to ward off my sexual jealousy, though she seemed genuine when she joked about making her shopping lists while they made love.

Lilian was impressive. She could think on her feet and talk in long, complex sentences; her face had good cheekbones, which she liked to point out in her favorite photos of herself, and a wide mouth with film star lips. Her humor often involved making fun of other people's stupidity; later, I would chafe against this, but for now being a special person in her life gave me a leg up. Sometimes at meetings her very words came out of my mouth and almost imperceptibly, our accents and vocabularies slid into each other's. "Bullshit!" I would exclaim. "Utter nonsense!" she'd snap.

We made a memorable couple with Lilian just over five feet and me six foot plus. Reveling in the item we'd become, we unveiled the news to an imagined drum roll at one of our consciousness raising meetings. So pleased were we with ourselves that we remained oblivious of Rosemary's pale unresponsiveness. Most of the others, though, were drawn to us as our bountiful sexual energy spilled over them like a blessing and they started dropping by in the afternoons when they knew Lilian would be at my flat. Like John and Oko, we held court in my sagging bed, a mattress I had bought for £1 on the King's Road and placed on top of plywood and concrete blocks. Lilian propped herself up on the pillows while one visitor or another sat in the big armchair eating her lunch and I lay under the quilt trying to enjoy the notoriety. It was an awfully long leap from secret, guilty sex.

We hadn't been together long when Lilian's husband gave her, as a present, a long weekend in Helsinki. Burdened by the conflict between her old life and the new direction in which she was headed, she had lobbied for a break from everything, including him, and he obliged, saying he would stay home with the children. Offering to drive her to the airport, I said somewhat dramatically that I would miss her every moment she was gone.

"Bring your passport—you never know," she said, refusing to elaborate.

The morning she was to leave, I was both hopeful and mystified.

"Park the car and come in with me," she ordered, as we swung into Heathrow. Then, at the tour company's check-in desk, she casually asked if there were any spaces left on the trip. Which is how I came to board the bright yellow plane that delivered us to three whole nights together in a king-size bed. We had never spent even one night together before, but now we ordered room service breakfast and even managed to leave the room a few times, once to search for a thick sweater to keep me warm and one evening to eat moose steaks with lingonberry sauce at a nearby restaurant. Reindeer wandered across the frozen bay and snowflakes drifted down past the streetlights as we hurried back to our room in a haze of sex. As far as I remember neither of us felt particularly uncomfortable at transforming Lilian's gift of alone time into an illicit weekend.

Later, when Lilian went to New York to visit her mother, I inexplicably thought nothing of spending the night with her next-door neighbor, a woman who'd been giving me the eye for a while. Somehow, I didn't think it had anything to do with Lilian and me, but Lilian certainly did, managing to intuit the whole thing over the phone. She accused me of being a faithless bitch and then, when she spotted me at the airport, burst into loud weeping which both embarrassed and terrified me. After that, whenever she and I tried for a special evening out at one of our favorite cheap restaurants, she cried into the goulash or the risotto. She didn't sob but simply wiped her chin when too much misery fell into her food.

"Take no notice of me," she'd demand, the hint of a tremble in her voice. I was so used to feeling responsible that it didn't occur to me her pain might not be caused by my infidelity alone. She must already have been suffering from the huge losses she knew lay ahead: a husband who'd been a good friend to her and children she was struggling to hold on to. It probably didn't occur to her, in turn, that I was perched precariously on top of my own unexamined mountain of loss. When we tried to discuss our future together, the weight of the past and the hectic pace of the unfolding present kept us from seeing beyond the daily round in which we were caught up.

The more she cried, the more desperate I was to comfort her and prove her wrong about me. I would stretch my hand across the table and wrap her small one in it and by the time we left I'd be eager to take her home and ease her clothes off. None of our wretchedness would enter the room where we made love. No matter what had gone on earlier, our bodies were reliably joyful together, dependably compatible in their eagerness. We laughed and tumbled, Lilian's long hair tickling my belly, our tongues re-exploring all the familiar places.

Lilian and I were together on and off throughout her coming out as a lesbian and losing custody of one of her children, though we were not exactly a couple, since couples weren't approved of by our comrades. Women who partnered up found neither encouragement to weather the difficulties that inevitably arose between them, nor any kind of discussion about how to nurture their relationships; such discussions were deplored as either selfish psychologizing or apolitical American bullshit, both of which were deemed to undermine a commitment to the community.

Our infatuation was intense for a while but had little chance of surviving. As was common in our circles, we dealt with our disillusionment by getting involved with other lovers. We seesawed between wanting a life together and acting as if we were single. Our wounds constantly bled but they eventually scarred over and we kept coming back for more. I had been Lilian's first woman lover, and she had been the first I fell for without secrecy. These firsts remained potent: our bodies stored them up—the texture of skin and hair, smells and tastes, sensations that refused to move aside in favor of other lovers who would surely have made for less tortured lives. It was always with relief that we wiped away each other's tears and unbuttoned our shirts.

BILLBOARDS AROUND town were being sabotaged with comments added by feminists. Jill Posener, a photographer, preserved for posterity many of these graffiti, such as the ad for a Fiat whose attractiveness was conveyed by the slogan: "If this car were a lady it would get its bottom pinched." Some enterprising woman had added in large, black lettering, "If this lady was a car, she'd run you down." Then there was the drastically simple one where a flirtatious woman advertised some tool or other under the heading "Renew his interest in carpentry." The riposte: "Saw his head off."

I suggested at one of our meetings that we take on the publicity campaign, aimed at a skeptical public, about the advantages of joining the European Economic Community. The decision needed to be made by Parliament but the business community, especially, had to be convinced. The billboards showed a man looking through a pair of binoculars across the English Channel to a French beach where two blond women with ballooning breasts and skimpy bikinis lounged invitingly. The caption read, "It's a better outlook into Europe."

"How could we ever find out where they all are?" Rosemary asked, her glasses wobbling on the end of her nose.

I'd learned a few useful things during my spell as an account executive at a London public relations firm. I called around and found out which advertising agency was in charge of the campaign. Posing as a reporter, I said: "We need to get some photos of people in the street giving their opinions in front of your poster. Can you point me to a few?"

At the next meeting, the group was satisfyingly impressed with the complete list I had picked up.

"Weren't you afraid they'd remember you later?" someone asked, echoing my anxiety.

"Don't be silly," Lilian said. "Nobody's going to investigate billboard defacement as if it's the Great Train Robbery!"

Soon we were huddled over the A to Zed, circling every location in red. But within two weeks, the group had lost interest in what had become my project and returned to its list of topics. Each week I brought up the posters and each week they reminded me that we hadn't yet tackled rape, the workplace, psychiatry, or motherhood, and, moreover, we were a discussion group, not a group of vandals. Some of them had good reasons, such as full-time jobs, for fearing arrest, and Lilian wasn't the only one with children at home. Still, I pursued my case even while my arguments trailed away, a jumble of unfinished sentences that floated upward like ladders with nowhere to set themselves down.

I couldn't let go of it. I longed to be among the rebels like those radical women in New York who had disrupted Miss World and staged a sit-in at the *Ladies Home Journal*. If the others wouldn't do it, then I would go alone. Once I'd decided, I wasted no time digging out the two cans of luminous green paint left by my flat's previous tenants and bought a spray gun from a hardware store across the river—well out of my neighborhood. A couple of evenings later, home alone after a quick spaghetti at the café below my flat, I paced around until it was dark and the street noise had faded away, then ran down the stone stairs and slopped some paint onto the car's back license plate: it would be hard to read if I was spotted. Wired and jittery by midnight, I was more excited than scared. I put on a navy roll-neck sweater and wool gloves and then paused to debate between heavy boots good for kicking and suede desert boots good for running. Running seemed more important. I loaded the supplies and set off.

The streets I knew so well assumed the dismal air of *film noir*. A man waiting for a cab on a street corner might well have just committed a murder. The rain that mizzled down on to the pavement surely obliterated bloody footprints. The roar of trucks on the overpass drowned out a scream or two. At the first billboard, I made myself jump out of the car before I had time to become paralyzed by my nerves, which were zinging like steel guitar strings. I wielded the sprayer as if it were a machine gun, landing more paint on myself than on the poster. When I pointed it upwards, the paint leaked back down my arms. My wool gloves were sodden and rapidly hardening; green footprints trailed behind me as I scurried back to the car, wondering how many pairs of those desert boots existed and whether I had worn my tread to an identifiable pattern.

I drove to the second location with blood whistling through my ears. Now I was beginning to feel scared. Pulling into the curb, I waited while people wandered by. A couple kissed endlessly right below the man with the binoculars, and a group of passing youths whistled and gestured at the rosy outlook into Europe.

When the street was finally empty, I sent an arc of dirty green across the French bimbos and tried to write "exploits women" at the bottom. Paint ran everywhere. My hair started to congeal in grayish clumps and irritation chased away my alarm. By the time I had done eight, I was worn out. A cup of coffee and a cigarette in Kilburn's Cozy All Night Caff would boost my resolve. But as I parked the car, I realized that I could hardly go in there with my hair paint-splattered, and the sleeves of my sweater hardening into green shells. Reluctantly, I decided to forego the coffee and do only one more: Shepherd's Bush Green would be the last.

I was heading west on Bayswater Road, coming up to the Esperanto Society, which I knew about because my grandfather had translated Shakespeare into Esperanto. Its windows were dark but I recognized it at the same moment as I realized I was driving way too slowly; cars were passing impatiently, some honking. A quick burst of a siren made me snap upright. The police car was flashing its beacon right on my tail.

Forcing myself to think strategically, I dragged two old sweatshirts from under the passenger seat and draped them over the paint can and sprayer as I pulled over. Slowly, the policeman got out of his car, shone his flashlight onto my license plate, and strolled up to my window. I was distinctly out of practice at flirting with men, but somehow summoned up my sweetest smile and did a bit of an eyelash flutter.

"License plate's not readable," he said, beaming the light into the car.

"Oh, I'm so sorry, officer," I said. "I was helping some friends decorate their flat and they messed around with the plate as I was leaving. I'll go right home and clean it off."

"Hmmm," he said. And then there was a long pause, during which he might or might not have heard my heart pounding.

"Better get along then, Missy. It's very late, you know." It was the Missy that confirmed it.

"Yes, officer. I will." And I did.

SOMEWHERE IN the middle of all this drama, I drove over the bridge to the Battersea Dogs Home where, hardening my heart to the howlers, the cringers, and the silent, almost tearful, older dogs, I snatched a wild-haired terrier mix from the jaws of euthanasia. Sheba sat on the car seat beside me with her head on my thigh and when we got home and I took a bath, she cried outside the door until I let her in. There she sat with her chin on the edge of the tub, gazing at me gratefully as she would continue to do for the next seventeen years.

I wasn't supposed to have a dog in the flat, but it was an easy rule to break, as the building was large and anonymous with no resident manager. Getting her outside to appropriate peeing spots was less easy; she insisted on grass for her morning outing though Pimlico was not rich in grass. In the end I resorted to lifting her over the low wall of a block of flats surrounded by lawns; there I slouched, smoking my first cigarette of the day and nonchalantly pretending to enjoy the morning air, while she snuffled around out of sight.

Sheba and I went to most of my meetings by car but when, occasionally, we needed to use the underground, we observed the signs that in those days were posted at the top of the escalators: "Dogs must be carried." This led to a trick, which we performed to admiring audiences: at the command "hup!" she would squat back on her haunches, look up at me from beneath her silver and black bangs, and leap from a standstill straight into my arms.

Once, Lilian, Zelda, and I took the red van to a conference in Bristol, the back filled with women and children sprawled on mattresses and Sheba curled up on a lap. On the last day, on our way back to London, we made a quick stop at the crèche to pick up someone's kid. Two hours later, at the first London drop-off, I discovered that Sheba was missing. I made everyone get out and drove back down the motorway, my stomach lurching, self-reproach mingling with horrible scenarios of Sheba wandering bedraggled through unfamiliar streets or perhaps lying injured beside the motorway.

It was dark when I pulled up outside the house where the crèche had been. There she was, sitting on the pavement under a streetlight, her head cocked to one side. When I drew up, she wagged her tail and more or less asked me what the fuck had happened to dinner.

Estranged as I was now from my family and old friends, and with lovers coming and going at bewildering speed, it was reassuring to know that I would always be the one Sheba would go home with.

VERONICA, LOIS, AND ME

EARLHAM STREET, Covent Garden, where the Women's Liberation Workshop had moved in 1974, was still mainly a warehouse district, interspersed with a few avant-garde performance spaces. I had been chosen as one of the four workers, not for my terrific skills but by the simple method of having my name drawn out of a hat, as well as being willing to forego the meager pay when there wasn't any money, which was most of the time. We workers welcomed newcomers to feminism who wandered in looking for something, as I had once done, something to change their lives. We also functioned, not very efficiently, as a clearinghouse for women's groups all over Britain, trying to keep track of what they were up to in Warwick and Manchester and numerous towns around the country.

My worst shifts were the ones I shared with Lois, who lamented over and over that the women's movement was in the hands of middle-class, white women—which of course it was. Lois was working class and proud of it. On Fridays, newsletter day, she and I assembled all the items we had received and organized them into some kind of sequence (it was office policy to print everything that was submitted without editing). Then, someone had to type the whole thing onto wax "dittos," which would be plastered on to the drum of the ancient machine, inked, and run off. The tension began around the typing: I had been sent to an expensive secretarial college, so I could type fast and accurately; Lois had had no such opportunity. However much I exhorted her to type the newsletter, she always claimed to be incapable and when I offered to teach her, she asked who I thought I was. So while I typed a list of upcoming events (Monday: Shrew Collective; Tuesday: Lesbian Liberation; Wednesday: Women's Abortion and Contraception Campaign, and so on), Lois threw out remarks like "the workers are the backbone of this country." Although I was working at the time, I knew she didn't mean me.

The centers of all the lowercase *a*'s, cut out by the typewriter, fell from personal ads, leaving black blobs in their place: ATTRACTIVE MALE GRADUATE *genuinely concerned with Women's Liber•tion required for light duties round • feminist fl•t*, or: HELPFUL CAT WANTED: *Going on holid•y? Home offered to • good mouse-c•tching c•t for 2 weeks*. On our worst days, ink spurted out, pages appeared upside down, and Rorschach designs obliterated poems and reports from the Night Cleaners' Campaign or the Disco Collective at The Crown and Woolpack. Lois threw her hands up and moaned. The denim overalls she wore every day remained unsullied, while I plunged in to extract a mutilated wax page, spreading ink up my arms and shirtfront. When finally I gave in and called the repairman, Lois glowered at both of us.

It was during this time that my old roommate, Veronica, surfaced. I'd met her when, at eighteen, I'd landed my first job and needed somewhere to live. At that time, it was common practice for young women to pack themselves into what had once been elegant Georgian homes, now converted into flats. One of the group, probably an experienced flat sharer, would hold the lease, often growing into something of a tyrant as a result of her responsibility for the payment of rent and the unpredictable comings and goings of her subtenants. Needing an immediate base not too far from Shepherd's Bush, I had called up "want to share" ads and soon found myself wandering along Kensington High Street, map in hand, searching for Melbury Road. Just past the entrance to Holland Park, I turned into the street of tall, brick houses with bay windows and narrow balconies. With a shiver of excitement, I imagined myself living there—a sophisticated Londoner setting off each morning to my job at the BBC's brand-new Television Centre.

The blue plaque on the house, when I found it, revealed it had once been occupied by the painter William Holman Hunt. The doorbell buzzed loudly when I fingered it, and Veronica Duncan, the lease-holder, opened the door cautiously and peered at me.

"I've come about the vacancy. We talked on the phone. I'm . . ."

"Well, you'd better come in then." She turned abruptly and trotted, as only a small woman can, up the stairs.

The flat, she told me, was home to six women—though we only spoke of "girls" back then—and consisted of three large, square rooms, two of which were bedrooms and one the sitting room, plus the kitchen and a messy bathroom.

"This is where you would sleep," she said, pointing to a single bed in the southeast corner of the room occupied by Veronica herself and a woman named Jo, who wandered in eating a banana. Her surreptitious wink was a reassuring antidote to Veronica's vexed explanation of how things worked. She pointed to the carved wardrobe next to what might become my bed and said, over her shoulder, "You can keep your food in there."

Dubiously, I eyed the ancient cupboard with its excess of curlicues before we marched on to the next stop of the tour. In the kitchen, where I might have expected the food to live, little was in evidence. Kitchen food, I was to discover, was fair game, even when labeled: Do NOT Eat This Jam—It Belongs To Lydia. Chocolate digestive biscuits, instant coffee, and tins of baked beans (all that any of us consumed) were stashed away under sweaters in drawers or in suitcases under beds.

Sharing a flat with Veronica was not easy. She was a walking bundle of irritations and ambitions. The irritations were usually directed at her five flatmates (rent late, food rotting, bath dirty); the ambitions were focused fair and square on the aristocracy. Veronica wanted an upper-crust husband, one she would meet at Ascot or the powerboat races frequented by playboy earls and viscounts. Accordingly, she was gone all day, working hard for a paycheck to cover the expensive suits and demure twin sets that made her look like the kind of girl those men's mothers wanted them to marry. Often, she had no money left for food.

We were all afraid of her temper, which would rise to spectacular heights when things got out of hand. Once, someone had an Australian friend camping out in the sitting room. Veronica, tormented by the mess, told him several times that he needed to move on until one Saturday morning she picked up armloads of his possessions and flung them over the balcony on to the street below. The last item, a red sleeping bag, floated down gracefully, a feather or two wafting away on the breeze, as Veronica turned to the astonished guest:

"Now perhaps you can get it through your thick head what leaving means," she snapped, turning on her heel to stalk into the bathroom, which was the only place you could slam a door with any hope of its staying slammed.

Pretty soon I moved on to a nicer flat with Jo and Lydia, never expecting to see Veronica again. It didn't occur to me that she might succeed in her pursuit of a blue-blooded husband, so I was stunned when I discovered that she had, indeed, snared one: Lord Lucan, known to his friends as "Lucky Lucan" because of his gambling. I could hardly reconcile that harried, tantrum-prone woman with the glittering Lady Lucan who started appearing on society pages. The lackluster skin I had seen coated with creams and face packs glowed in the reflection of dazzling necklaces; the once-stringy blond hair flew out in a cloud as she rode in what might have been an Aston Martin.

MY JOB at the workshop guaranteed that I heard about virtually everything in feminist London, especially the more bizarre events, and

Veronica's showing up at a socialist feminist meeting was one of the most bizarre. When the women there discovered she was Lady Lucan, the grapevine reported that she'd been subjected to a barrage of interrogation about the class system as if she herself had invented it.

Veronica had told them she was powerless. Her title meant nothing. She had no bank account. No way of escaping. Although she wanted to divorce Lord Lucan, who she claimed was violent, she was afraid he would get custody of their children. His family had all the influence; she had none. But she did still have a lovely house in Belgravia where her husband no longer lived. She offered to let the feminists use it for meetings.

This story rapidly made the rounds. Women passed it along to others in the bookshop or on the stairs to the meeting room; phone calls lobbed it from Hammersmith to Hackney. But Veronica's appearance in my world made me uneasy. What kind of idiot would admit to having had a connection with the aristocracy, no matter how long ago— no matter that it was before the lady in question got herself ennobled. Even if I made it clear that I'd never particularly liked her, mightn't I inadvertently reveal some remnant of the snobbery that had been instilled in me, in all of us middle-class girls I dare say. I kept my head down and hoped the topic would run out of steam.

Jacky wandered in as she often did after her day as an accountant at a nearby office. Unlike the unemployed women who hung around all day at the workshop—the political watchdogs, trendsetters, and youthful leaders of popular, though not always intelligent, opinion—Jacky was a grown up. She didn't mind appearing in her decent clothes or objecting to the latest outrageous mandate. Nor was she afraid to let her round face relax into genuine friendliness when she liked a person or an idea, even if all those around her were hedging their bets behind neutrality or preemptive disapproval. She could be relied on, too, for the practical approach, especially when ambitious plans were being floated for nationwide campaigns or international conferences. Jacky was invariably the one to count the cost, to weigh up the pluses and minuses.

Over a couple of pints at the pub around the corner, I confided in her about the Melbury Road flat, emphasizing how quickly I had moved on with the two who had become my friends. Jacky nodded, apparently unsurprised. We should get in touch and commiserate with Veronica's situation, she said; at the very least we should thank her, on behalf of the movement, for the offer of her house, which we knew would never be taken up.

Considering this, I drained my tankard and stood up to buy another round. But Jacky hadn't finished: I would be the perfect person since I was a movement worker and had also once known her.

"Oh, she won't remember me," I said quickly.

"Yeah, right," she said, giving me a look.

WEAK SUNSHINE broke through as Jacky and I pulled up and plugged the parking meter. When I rapped there was a long wait. Finally, Veronica appeared and hustled us in.

A partly open door, a glimpse of a formal dining room wallpapered in maroon, and then we were shooed into a large drawing room furnished with wing armchairs and slender-legged antique side tables. Sunbeams slanted through motes of dust, which hovered expectantly in the air. A portrait of an earlier Earl of Lucan, a baby-faced man in a red jacket, hung over the fireplace.

The room was messy enough to be almost familiar, yet the bleakness underneath the clutter was nothing like the untidiness at my shared house. Here, the slippers, newspapers, piles of mail, dirty plates, and pizza boxes that littered the surfaces and much of the floor, revealed a life taken over by hopelessness. For a moment, I recalled the chaos of the flat where Veronica had often referred to the rest of us as "a bunch of filthy pigs," though that felt inappropriate to think about now as I took in the full extent of her deterioration. Emaciated, she looked as if she weighed perhaps ninety pounds. Her hair hung in clumps and needed washing. Her trouser suit was stained with coffee and, judging from the jumbled blankets on the couch, she'd been sleeping in this room.

Jacky and I sat on the window seat while Veronica talked. She spoke compulsively, frantically, as if her life depended on saying everything.

"He's mad you know—completely mad. He wants to get the children . . . thinks I'm not good enough to bring them up properly . . . finally I said we had to separate and he moved into the mews around the corner. He went over the edge, you know . . . not that he wanted to stay with me . . . he's always furious when I try to go to the club with him . . . but he just hates to let me stay here alone . . ."

I felt myself grow numb, floating somewhere distant even while I noted the classic symptoms that feminists had so recently put a name to: Veronica—a battered wife? Yes, she was. She began to describe Lucan's physical violence, his beatings and sexual attacks to the accompaniment of Nazi marching songs. It all struck me as utterly over the top but her agitation and pain were such that I leaned forward and gripped my knees.

Veronica took a gulp of air, forcing herself into the present moment, and looked around, dazed.

"Oh, I'm so sorry," she said in an incongruously high hostess voice. "I don't have anything to offer you. There's no food and I have no money."

"No money?" said Jacky, astonished.

"Oh, I don't need to eat much," Veronica said vaguely. "I can't get any money out of the bank because he's put some kind of a stop on it. And I don't have any money of my own." When feminists had described women's economic dependence on men, I'd never pictured a milieu like this.

We deferred to the agitated woman and allowed her to do the only thing she could: she telephoned Harrods, where apparently the Earl had forgotten to cancel her account, and ordered a large pizza. As the delivery boy sped away towards Victoria Station, Veronica grabbed a slice and bit off a chunk. Then she put it down on the arm of her chair and forgot it, all the while telling us about Lucan's dreadful gambling debts and how his friends had ganged up against her. Every once in a while, she would pick up another slice from the box and take a bite until the tables and chairs around her were strewn with half-eaten pieces. Once I stretched across and took a piece myself, but when Veronica flopped onto the blankets with a stifled sob, I put it down with her leftovers.

Jacky and I stood up. I wondered if I should go over to Veronica. But what would I do? She would hardly allow me to hug her or even hold her hand. I recognized her acute need of comfort and I knew, too, that it existed alongside a horror of being pitied. Probably someone braver and more spontaneous than I could have gathered her up with loving arms, but I told myself that it would only upset her if she had to show us the face she had buried in the cushions. Her muffled whimpering died away and she remained sprawled, corpse-like on the sofa.

"Do call if we can do anything," Jacky said on her way out of the room. "Yes," I echoed weakly, "do call."

CLOSE TO a year had passed when one evening, ambling through the late shift at the workshop, I picked up a paper someone had left lying around. At first the headline might have been just the normal *Evening Standard* hyperbole: BLOODY MURDER! ESCAPE IN THE NIGHT!—that sort of thing. Then I noticed Lord Lucan's name. The police were hunting for the Earl of Lucan, who had not been seen since his children's nanny was found the previous night, battered to death at the family's home. Lady Lucan had also been viciously attacked and, although beaten bloody, she had escaped and run to the nearby Plumbers Arms for help.

"Blimey!" I gasped, staring at a picture dug up from newspaper files.

I called Jacky, continuing to read the article as I dialed. She had already seen it.

"She's in hospital," she said.

"Her children were upstairs all the time," I said, "and he—"

"Yes, yes, I know. Stop rabbiting on."

We must once again reach out to Veronica, Jacky said. But if I'd been reluctant to get mixed up with Veronica when she was merely an inconvenient relic of my past, now it felt frightening.

"Listen," I said, "Mightn't it be a good idea to find out where the rabid Lucan has gone to earth before we jump in?" It would be mighty unpleasant, I pointed out, to encounter the lead pipe, which had killed the nanny and bloodied Veronica. Jacky thought for a moment then agreed that we should wait.

That night my mattress felt lumpier than usual and the November air was chilly. Throwing blankets off and pulling them on again, I remembered the big bedroom where Veronica used to curl up in her corner. She never moved and hardly even breathed; certainly no snores ever came from her direction although Jo, in the other corner, sometimes grunted or let out a snort. Had Veronica really been unconscious or was she perhaps rehearsing the refined sleep that might be required when she moved up in the world? I saw Veronica's bare legs and her small, white feet; I watched her kick away her slippers and run in a blur of speed; there was terror in those feet as drops of blood from her head spattered across the buttery sandstone of a Belgravia pavement.

For a couple of days, the papers were full of revelations. Lucan had been living just around the corner in Eaton Row and was trying to get custody of their children. On the night of the murder he had visited a friend, talked to his mother, and then gone out gambling. Although it was supposed to have been the nanny Sandra Rivett's night off, she had stayed home. She was short and thin like Veronica and, attacked in the dark, most likely had been mistaken for her; when Veronica had gone to see what all the noise was about, she too had been assaulted. If he were caught, since he could only be tried by a jury of his peers, there would be a rare and sensational trial in the House of Lords. Then the car he had borrowed that day was found with a piece of blood-soaked lead pipe in the boot, near the port of Newhaven; presumably he'd escaped to France. The police alerted Interpol with the message, "Wanted for murder and attempted murder: Richard John Bingham, 7th Earl of Lucan. Please arrest. Extradition will follow."

A few nights later, I had a dream about Veronica. A ship crowded with upper-class twits was steaming straight towards a rocky reef with Lady Lucan looking desperately back from the stern. It occurred to me when I awoke that she and I now had something in common: the daily scrutiny and speculation by strangers of a painful story in our lives. When the cruise ship my parents were on had caught fire and an international rescue effort was underway I, too, had had to watch my story unfold on TV, on front pages and on hoardings, along with everyone else in Britain.

Almost every day Jacky dropped in, speculating about Veronica, who reportedly had left St George's Hospital and was in hiding with a detective keeping watch. She wouldn't give up bugging me about writing to Veronica and I began to wish she'd find something else to do, but Jacky had the gift of getting her way through quiet persistence. So I agreed to compose another note.

"Do you think she really gets her letters?" I wondered as we jotted down a few sympathetic sentences.

"Probably the detectives read everything in case . . ." She trailed away, but I knew the rest: in case the lunatic tried to lure her to some remote place where he could finish her off. They most certainly ought to be monitoring her mail.

Since sending a letter would invite police attention to our political circles, we decided to go to the house and deliver it directly, though why this seemed preferable escapes me now; we didn't even know if Veronica was there. We included both our home phone numbers and sealed the note in an envelope. Then we drove through a heavy downpour to 46 Lower Belgrave Street where the door was opened immediately by a man in a shiny suit, whom I took to be a detective. Rain was plastering my hair to my face.

"I'd like to see Lady Lucan," I said, trying to appear entitled to whatever I wanted. I figured that's what he would expect of a friend of Veronica's.

"She's not available," he said curtly. "And I'd like your name, please, and that letter for Lady Lucan too."

I ended up giving him my name and address, as well as the note. As we drove away, I crossed my fingers and hoped that Veronica would never call us.

The murder became the *cause célèbre* it remains to this day. Public opinion settled on the theory, confirmed at an inquest, that Lucan killed Sandra Rivett by mistake, intending Veronica as his victim. There was a warrant out for his arrest and sales of *I've Seen Lord Lucan* T-shirts were brisk as sightings popped up all over the world, especially in South Africa and the West Indies. At the inquest, a lone woman walked up and down outside the Coroner's Court holding up her sign: "It affects us all, rich and poor."

There was a steady stream of articles about Lucan's "distinguished" background, invariably mentioning the great-great-grandfather who took part in the Charge of the Light Brigade and the great-grandfather who had assisted at the Coronation of King Edward VII. There were also exposés of his full-time professional gambling at the Clermont Club, where he hung out with friends who grumbled about the state of England, deploring the fact that white skin no longer held sway. Many of these friends proposed hanging or flogging foreigners and some had joined private armies, advocating a military coup, or so it was reported later.

Over time it came out that Lucan had been on the verge of bankruptcy and was making plans to sell the family silver. As a boy, he'd finagled the money to pay for Eton when his parents, who were among that rare breed—upper-class socialists—would have sent him to a grammar school. In one of his many efforts to hit the big time, he'd taken a screen test to become the new James Bond but he turned out to be more suited to real-life dissipation than Hollywood derring-do.

Towards the end, with his legendary luck running out, he'd set off grimly, day after day, to Berkeley Square where he ate salmon and lamb cutlets for lunch and threw away the last of his fortune at *chemin de fer*.

AFTER DELIVERING the note, we heard nothing from Veronica, but Jacky and I continued to send notes, gifts of food, and suggestions. As I compiled lists of counselors, shelters, discussion groups, my neck tightened and a headache took root. I knew there wasn't anything we could offer Veronica; her title, and the manner she had acquired with it, pushed far too many buttons in our circles.

Once, I reached her on the phone and she said, "Oh, good Lord, Judy, I couldn't possibly send my children to a state school! I have to ensure a proper upbringing for them," which I knew meant schools—very expensive schools—where her kids would play with the royals. Although she was, in fact, destitute, she didn't act poor; her status was the one thing she had left to hold on to, and she wasn't about to relinquish it. Neither Jacky nor I could be sure she would be treated well by any feminist group—or that she, in turn, would treat them decently.

I steered the conversation to the women's movement and the meeting she'd gone to. "They were dreadfully scruffy," she complained. "Some of them were even lesbians." I was aware of her exaggerated, plummy accent and my own, which now had become something closer to that of a London dockhand than of a Sussex girl educated at a private school. BBC accents were rapidly disappearing; even the Americans among us were perfecting glottal stops. "Go' uh copy of the newsle'a?" they would ask, with a faint remnant of Boston or New York under the staccato.

I wasn't sorry to drop her. Jacky called two or three more times, but when she got no answer, she too lapsed and Veronica faded from view. Every now and then, though, Lois, puffing up the stairs to join me on the morning shift, would bring up the scandal. It was a scab she couldn't resist scratching.

"Anything new about that Lucan woman?" she would ask, filling the kettle and trying to sound casual. I knew she was poised to strike, no matter what I said.

In Lois's view, poverty was more than an absence of money: it was a lifestyle, an attitude, a working-class culture—one where I didn't belong. No matter how rough my accent, how meager my shrinking bank account, Lois and I would never—at least not in Britain in the 1970s—find a way into each other's worlds.

"I can't believe she refused your 'elp," Lois grumbled in a rare moment of solidarity with me. "Her Ladyship's just too good for the likes of *us*."

ELGIN AVENUE

THE TALL, terraced house with a purple front door at 98 Elgin Avenue was so famous that no one ever referred to its number; they simply said, What's going on at Elgin these days? By the time I moved in, in 1974, it was one of the best-known strongholds of the lesbian separatists, where ten or eleven women had been living for more than a year, many passing through for a week or a month with a core group of five or six holding fast. It was a squat—an empty house that had simply been entered and settled into—but soon it would be recognized as a women's housing association, its members permitted by the Greater London Council to occupy all except the basement, which had a sitting tenant, until such time as the authorities might snatch it back for upgrading.

The door was opened by a woman whose face, in the November sun, blended the chiseled bones of a Pre-Raphaelite beauty with the strong jaw line of a New York Jew. I recognized the momentary search for an appropriate gesture that flashed across her face (shaking hands was so male); our eyes met when she solved the dilemma with a friendly touch on my upper arm.

Deborah, I would soon discover, was a diplomatic handler of squabbles. She was the only one who had managed to befriend Doris, the basement's longtime occupant, whose life was mightily disturbed by our carryings-on. Deborah placated her with gifts of chocolate chip cookies, the most elaborate product ever to emerge from our kitchen. When she wasn't soothing Doris's ruffled feelings or picking her way around the dirty dishes to make herself a bean sprout salad, she drew perceptive pen and ink portraits of the women who came and went.

A hint of rose water hovered around her ground floor front room, where she spent a lot of time with the door shut; if the door were to stand open, I could glimpse the portraits tacked up on the wall and propped along the mantle. When she emerged, she'd have her beige knitted hat pulled down to her eyebrows, which had something to do with the fact that she had had a brain tumor that nearly killed her, though I never heard her mention it and only learned about it much later. I remembered then how once or twice I'd seen her pause on the stairs and put her hand on the wall as if she were dizzy.

I scored a tall, square room behind Deborah's. Both rooms suffered from their location. All through the night women arrived home, slammed the door, and thumped up the staircase, whose wooden steps had been energized with remnants of leftover paint: three or four treads scarlet, a whole flight brown, and the rest navy with one canary yellow riser shining near the half-landing, where the bathroom door stood permanently open.

I dumped my duffel bag on the floor and started to hang up flannel shirts on a makeshift rail from which dangled a few hangers. The alcove behind it had been painted a dark plum color and the dirty white of the other walls had holes where chunks of plaster had fallen away from drawing pins. Tape marks crisscrossed the corners of phantom posters. I set up my fan heater, which reared up on its metal stand and puffed warm air into the chilly vault, rattling noisily on the uncarpeted floor. (Doris no doubt rolled her eyes towards her ceiling; the next morning she would corner me by the front gate and give me the first of many lectures about floor noise.)

Sheba curled up on an old quilt under the table in front of the boarded-up fireplace. Someone had, in an earlier era, painted the table black, though by now the paint had chipped, leaving the original gloss only on the insides of its sturdy legs, as if all beauty had worn away except from those most private inner thighs. I placed my blue portable Remington dead center with an unopened ream of paper next to it. Whenever I opened the door, it squatted there on the wide tabletop, waiting like another faithful dog.

The school playground, directly behind our untended, postage-stamp of a garden, hurled its yells towards my window at recess, and twice a week the school's steel band drummed a muddle of harmonies. When the children were gone, even with the incessant background noise of the house—women striding, bounding, shuffling from room to room, and the occasional outburst of song or anguish—my room wrapped its walls around a particular quietness. If I stayed very still, I thought I could hear it breathe and that breathing was the most comforting intimacy I found there, even though, like everyone else's, my arms were always hungry, always reaching out to hold somebody.

The old mattress I'd bought on the King's Road arrived in the She Can Do It van, along with my mother's Parker Knoll wing chair. This, together with her well-loved Grundig radiogram, were whisked upstairs and added to the motley assortment of furniture in the sitting room. Meanwhile, I wrestled the mattress into a corner, although this time I didn't have any boards or concrete blocks to hold it up, so it was uncomfortable to sit on for conversational purposes. This became clear when Heather, who had recently arrived from Australia with her friend Eunice, dropped by that first evening to see how the room and I were getting on.

Her almost inaudible knock was as restrained and polite as she herself was. Her dark, straight hair framed her face and her slightly wide-eyed gaze was calm, as it would remain even when turmoil erupted around her. "Can I come in, Judy?" She leaned in the doorway, assessing my response.

"How are you?" she asked, the rise of her voice on the word "are," revealing a genuine question, not just a preamble. On the makeshift bed, we sat together and talked. Eventually we tipped over and stretched out, kissing tentatively, as if it were really the fault of the mattress and its lack of a backrest.

After that, she came quite often. Sometimes there was just the murmur of our voices and our heads close together on my pillow; other times I would feel myself falling into Heather's languid lovemaking. After that happened two or three times, I was surprised to discover that it hadn't grabbed me or stabbed me as sex so often did—I wasn't seized by an unstoppable urge to rush up to the top floor and see what Heather was up to or who she was with; I wasn't even waiting for the next time. Weeks would go by but sooner or later there'd be another knock. Sex with Heather was simply a conversation that turned from talk to touch.

IT WAS impossible not to hear Cath and Llyn's dramas that periodically erupted up on the third floor, threats and tears spilling down the stairs into the kitchen and sitting room. Cath was a doctor who had exchanged a drug-addicted boyfriend for Llyn, who cycled through alcohol binges, withdrawals, and relapses.

The first time I found myself alone in the kitchen with Llyn, I was apprehensive as I watched her blacken two pieces of toast under the grill and slather them with butter and marmalade, then knock back two mugs of Nescafé with a lot of sugar and no milk.

"That's better," she said, "I feel halfway human now—well, halfway womanish, I suppose." She grinned a slightly wicked grin, pulling me into one of the fleeting alliances we all formed when we made fun of ourselves.

As we debated the ending of Nelly Kaplan's film, *La Fiancée du Pirate*, and the merits of Carly Simon's album, *Anticipation*, Llyn refilled the kettle three times and showed no sign of becoming the scary person who yelled and threw things at the wall. I pulled my green sleeping sweater down over my pajamas and relaxed into liking her. The smell of alcohol that had been clinging to her skin was gradually replaced by her Drum tobacco exhalations as she rolled cigarette after cigarette and spooned more sugar into her mug. I ran my fingers through my tangled curly hair and watched her eyes dart around the room and her hands sweep upwards as she argued with speedy eloquence. It was as if her words and gestures could hardly keep up with her mind.

Some of Elgin's social life took place in the spacious bathroom. The high-water mark and yellow mineral stains had long since become permanent features of the tub, over one end of which loomed an antique geyser. I discovered the hard way how long to let the hot tap run before lighting the gas: if you got it wrong, it would explode with a great whoosh and blow soot off its top; and if you happened to be sitting there, anticipating the delicious creep of hot water up your shivering, naked body, you would immediately resemble a chimney sweep. Next to the bath was a white wicker chair with once-flat arms that sagged where many elbows had rested; the bather's visitor could lounge there, reading aloud from the workshop newsletter or sharing her anxiety about money or politics, menstrual cramps or the state of the kitchen.

One day not long after I'd moved in, I had the chair while Euni lay in the tub, her ample breasts bobbing in front of her. Heather sat in the corner on the floor reading a crumpled copy of *Off Our Backs*. Rather diffidently, though with a faint undercurrent of annoyance, Euni splashed her feet and observed that I wasn't spending much time in the house.

"Don't you like us?" she asked, her voice climbing half an octave. Heather looked up. I blushed, aware that I'd been given what was considered a nice room and that others might be eyeing it with envy. I also understood that it was impossible to create a real community if the proportion of permanent residents to casual drop-ins was out of kilter. Up to now, I'd been wavering somewhere between the two, although I did sincerely want to take my place in the life of the house. The problem was Lilian.

She and I were tightly and chaotically bonded, our connection knotting us into a sexual, possessive, and utterly untenable snarl. As soon as I moved into Elgin, Lilian professed to dislike most of my housemates. Apart from Deborah, the only one she approved of was wild-haired Sandy, with whom she'd founded a Jewish lesbian group, but Sandy was fast retreating with a new lover, a woman who not only distinguished herself from the rest of us by having a real job but found the semi-squalor in which we lived distasteful.

Lilian declared all the others boring, self-centered, or lacking in radical verve. I knew this was a cover for the painful reality of my sleeping around—which she was doing too. We didn't "believe in monogamy," as it was phrased then, just as one might not believe in capitalism: both were considered to be an integral part of the patriarchy we intended to dismantle, a stance that did not preclude good old-fashioned jealousies. Unwilling to run into any of the women she suspected I'd slept with, Lilian insisted that if we were to spend the night together, we must sleep at her flat.

I was actually keen to move in with Lilian, but she thought that having a lesbian mother was quite enough for her teenage daughter, who still lived at home, to cope with. That was for her to decide, I said, but if I couldn't live with her, then I had to live somewhere else and she ought to be willing to come over to my place, at least sometimes.

She wouldn't budge. One evening, after dinner at her flat, I told her that I was on the way to getting a migraine and needed to head home.

Not having grasped the concept of Elgin Avenue as anybody's real home, she thought of it as a nest of sexually predatory vipers. "Don't go, Jude," she pleaded sweetly as she dried and put away the dishes.

When I didn't answer, she tipped the dirty dishwater down the drain and casually dropped the name of Mo into the conversation. Mo was a short, tough butch with a crewcut, who periodically pursued Lilian. I shoved aside images of my lover and Mo tangled in each other's arms, gave her a quick kiss, and left.

Some hours later I was asleep when the phone rang upstairs. It was not unusual for calls to come at night, sometimes from a woman who'd been arrested and needed bailing out, more often from someone in another country who couldn't count the time zones. There was a knock at my door and a grumpy voice, "It's Lilian. For you."

This would not be the last time that Lilian called Elgin at two or three in the morning, weeping and hysterical, sometimes even hinting that she was suicidal. At these moments our dramas rivaled those of Cath and Llyn, and my housemates, at least those who could wake up, dragged themselves down to the kitchen and brewed a pot of tea.

"I'd better go over there," I'd say, feeling something like a tidal wave curl over my head.

"No," Heather would say, "don't fall for it. Stay here with us."

But staying with them wouldn't ease what gnawed inside me. Was it fear of losing Lilian or fear of committing to her? More often than not, I went.

OLLY MOVED into the passage-like room behind mine, though I didn't run into her for a week or two. When I did, she emerged into the hall-way wearing baggy jeans and a black bowler hat jammed down so hard that the rim pushed the tops of her ears forward, lending her a touch of Prince Charles. She grabbed hold of the wobbly newel post at the bottom of the stairs and looked me up and down.

"I've been reading Djuna Barnes all day," she confided in a growly voice.

I felt my face flush. Who was June—or had she said Oona?—Barnes? I was used to my body sending out these signals when confronted with my ignorance. I nodded and retreated to my room but began to eye her whenever she appeared. It wasn't the bowler that made her intrigu-ing; it wasn't even the careless cut of her jeans; it was how comfortably she dwelled inside her butch skin.

We had not yet heard of baby butches, soft butches, stone butches, or lipstick lesbians, and transgender would come along much later. We recognized queer only as an epithet hissed or hurled at us on the street. Butch and femme were rejected as passé, since we thought they imitated heterosexuality and reeked of a time when lesbians had to hide. We were going to be whatever we damn well wanted to be. Yet I think most of us suspected there was something to the notion of butch and femme; we couldn't fail to notice that femmes ended up with butches and butches with femmes.

It was not about the clothes: in flannel shirts and jeans the femmes looked femmy and the butches looked butch. Later, when it was okay for butches to stomp around in leather, trailing chains, or for femmes to drape themselves in flowing materials with bits of underwear slipping from their shoulders, then a stranger might have thought it was about clothes, but it was not. Nor was it about assertiveness. Lilian was far more assertive than me, to put it mildly, and all my other lovers were too. I might have claimed, though, that it is usually the butch who takes responsibility for making a sexual relationship happen. This was not necessarily the same thing as instigating actual sex: it had more to do with making romance a possibility in the other's mind—more, some would say, with taking the first risk. Femmes would probably have disagreed with this, claiming to have played a major role in getting things going—and who's to say they were wrong? All I knew was that their method was different from the butch method and I didn't recognize it.

Somewhere in my pre-feminist years, I'd got hold of *The Well of Loneliness* and met Radclyffe Hall's heroine, Stephen Gordon, who considered herself a Man-Trapped-in-a-Woman's-Body. This didn't explain me, nor did it explain those women who lusted after the Men-Trapped-in-Women's-Bodies. In spite of the dreary plots of the cheap romance paperbacks I read in secret, I knew those femmes were not just heterosexual victims, lured into the twilight world of the M-T-I-A-W-Bs against their better judgment. They were every bit as lesbian as the butches. Only much later did I understand that there *are* people who feel trapped in the wrong body, people we now call transgender. But for myself, once I realized that I didn't have to be girly, I felt exquisitely female.

I'd never wanted to be a boy. My childhood careened through days of roller skating, horse riding, tree climbing, kick the can, swimming, tennis, and the construction of forts, grass huts, tree houses, miniature stables, and show-jumping courses for the family dachshunds. Every weekday I tied the knot of my uniform school tie and straightened the white collar under which it lay. Once in a while, when I was invited to a birthday party, my mother would cajole me into a dress and I'd feel like one of those chimpanzees that weird couples on television adopt and gussy up in frilly skirts and hair ribbons.

On winter days in my bedroom with the door closed against my mother, rain beating against the windows, time slowed down as I recounted in red exercise books the adventures of my stuffed horse, Peter. Wrapped in a blanket, I transformed Peter from a stubborn colt into a world-class show jumper. Along the way, he encountered cruel masters like the villains in *Black Beauty* and tender girls who recognized his innate brilliance and restored him to health. Cheap blue Biro ink smudged the pages and stained my fingers as I scribbled through four notebooks and Peter achieved his retirement in a lush meadow. The great thing about those hours with the red notebooks was that there was genderlessness, as well as timelessness, in the act of writing.

AS THE leaves turned to mulch and mud spread through Elgin's hallway, I wrote in notebooks and typed up poems, other women's as well as my own, to pin on the wall by my bed. Their rhythms flowed through my arms and fingers as I struck the keys. If a line break seemed wrong, my fingers would type right on over it and I'd have to go back, x out the run-on words, and slam the carriage return lever to start a new line. I wouldn't have dared interfere with another poet's work, but my fingers noticed when it didn't feel quite right.

The wall beside my mattress sprouted yellowing sheets of paper: not just the poems but also pithy quotes and pieces of *I Ching* wisdom from Lilian, who consulted the oracle daily. Upstairs, someone was invariably on the phone conducting a muttered conversation. She would be hunched in the space between the black payphone on the wall and the sitting room door, leaning against the shelf where the house kitty in its metal box waited hopefully for some gas-bill money. Sometimes it was Cath, looking distressed, in which case she was probably trying to locate Llyn. If it was someone setting out on a marathon talk, she might have dragged a kitchen chair out there and settled herself under the larger-than-life Judy Chicago print: a bloody tampax nosing its way out of a gaping vagina, anonymous fingers pulling on the string.

I knew my housemates in the way you know women you encounter in their pajamas with crusted drool on one cheek, but I knew almost nothing of where they'd come from—our conversations addressing only today, tomorrow, or an unspecified but better future. Our focus was the movement and working out how to live agreeably with a dozen women, some of whom were, or had been, or might become, one's lovers (which to us, was not separate from, but an intrinsic part of the movement). While my consciousness raising group had been focused on the past, or at least the parts of our pasts that matched the list of topics we were working through, at Elgin we moved on from all that. When we linked arms, six abreast, marching down Oxford Street, Whitehall, or around Trafalgar Square, jubilantly kicking out our toes behind a lesbian banner, it didn't matter where we'd sprung from. We were women who refused to live in dead-end jobs, pornographic films, or dull or abusive marriages. Our public presence refuted the nonsense of the bitter lesbian so often revealed at the end of novels to be the traitor or the poison pen letter writer.

When we drummed and shouted "Two, four, six, eight, what do we appreciate?" the answers ran the gamut from "freedom!" to "angry women!" to "dykes!"

"Here come the feminists!" we chanted. "We are your worst nightmare."

WITHOUT THE perks from my job in the family business, I couldn't afford a car and bought a motorbike. Or that's what I told myself; probably I just wanted to be the kind of lesbian who owned a motorcycle. I'd never driven or even ridden on the back of one since I was seven, when my brother had let me wrap my arms around his waist to zoom in and out of traffic along the North Circular Road, but there I was, in Camberwell, writing a check and being handed the keys to a Honda 500, which I had chosen only for its lovely sky-blue tank.

"Would you show me how it works?" I asked the dealer.

The man, all in leather, looked incredulous. But he obligingly threw his leg over the machine, pulled in the clutch with his left hand and demonstrated gear shifting: one down and three up with the left toe. Then, smiling at me through uneven teeth, he explained about the accelerator and brakes.

"Better 'op on and give it a try, love," he said, dismounting, looking dubious.

I snapped the strap of my new red helmet under my chin, twisted the throttle, revved the engine, clicked into first gear, and bounded across the forecourt like a kangaroo.

The diciest part of the ride home was negotiating Hyde Park Corner, where buses loomed over me, taxis advanced menacingly, and there was no space at all to sidle into the circling mass of metal. I hovered on the periphery like a kid on the playground poised to jump into a skipping rope. Cars hooted and bore down until I thought there would never be an opening, but it was the cycle that finally took the plunge when I inadvertently let the clutch out and we hopped in front of a black limo. I leaned low over the handlebars as I raced north and turned onto Elgin Avenue, then parked by the front gate and swaggered up the path, swinging my helmet.

I named the bike Gloria in honor of the glorious sensation of speed she gave, as well as for her color, which reminded me of the early blooms of a morning glory. The next day, an office supply shop provided several packages of silver stars, which I stuck all over the blue tank.

For a while, Gloria added zest to the unpredictable course of my love life as well as a prominent role in a poster that became famous in feminist circles. Lilian's hair whirled out exuberantly beneath the spare helmet on the morning we set off for a demolition site somewhere in the grungy part of Paddington to meet the half dozen others who would be in the photo. Jewell, the woman behind this project, had rented real guns from the army, which required a perplexed soldier to hand out machine guns with fixed bayonets and watch as we positioned ourselves in the window spaces and doorways of a crumbling wall, across which the title of the poster was scrawled in thick, red paint: "The Women's Army is Marching." I was in the foreground, astride my motorcycle, gun propped on my thigh, bayonet pointing skyward.

We were not intending to take up arms. The militant scenario was a fanciful conceit although we did intend it to communicate that we meant business. Guns were not at all common in England; we thought that to pose with them looking tough would be shocking. A few weeks later, the poster appeared on walls all over London. The postcard version started winging its way to destinations far and wide, no doubt shooting off messages like "Happy birthday sweetie," or "Sorry I was such an ass," or "I'm off to the Ashram: take care of the cat."

WHEN JANUARY blew in, a thin layer of ice coated the inside of my window each morning, filtering the light like the frosted glass of a Victorian front door and blurring the tree trunk outside until it might have been a shady visitor with a trilby hat pulled down over his eyes. The space heater vibrated all the time and I knew that Doris was lying in wait for me. A couple of days earlier, she'd rushed up the basement steps, rolling like a barge in a choppy sea. Puffing to a halt, she'd steadied herself against a pillar, shopping bag in hand. "Just a minute, you," she said. She had never mastered my name. This time, it was also about my boots. "I can hear 'em, one after the other. What do you do, throw 'em up to the ceiling and let 'em fall, *plonk, plonk,* right over my bed?"

I promised to undress more cautiously and stand my heater on two folded blankets. She shrugged her shoulders right up to her ears, squeezing her eyes shut and screwing up her face as if in pain. Then she sailed back down to her domain, swaying from foot to foot.

The cold weather brought an invasion of mice. I heard them scurrying around at night, tiny toenails scratching the floorboards while I lay on the mattress hoping they wouldn't burrow into my bed. One day, I wandered into the kitchen for my morning cuppa and greeted Lesley, our newest housemate, who was standing hopefully over the toaster—a recent acquisition intended to prevent the conflagrations that came with toasting bread under the grill. Since she was the only other nonvegetarian in the house, I'd been planning to suggest that we go down the road together for a bacon sandwich, but before I could speak, I noticed the box of corn flakes on the table moving. I rubbed my eyes and looked again. Yes, it was, gathering momentum as it tilted further and further to each side, about to topple over.

"Mouse!" I said, pointing. Lesley grunted and pulled out her toast. By the time she sat down, the packet was wobbling drunkenly towards her side of the table.

"I'll take it outside and drown it," she said matter-of-factly, squeezing the top closed and getting up. But at that moment Cath arrived in the doorway tossing back her limp, brown hair. The slight lisp, which marked her everyday speech, disappeared.

"We must save the sweet mouse," she declared, her *s*'s decidedly crisp. Then, as Llyn stepped in from the hallway and Heather and Euni ran downstairs to see what was going on, Cath seized the packet and summoned us all into the sitting room. Lesley raised one eyebrow at me as we settled in our pajamas, overcoats, and scarves around the oil storage heater and blew into our hands. Cath held the box protectively on her lap.

"We can't just let it go in the house," somebody said, as if there weren't already mice running in and out, possibly hundreds of them. Heather, who would later return to Australia and start a refuge for injured animals, offered to help Cath suss out a good place to release the animal while Lesley, hardly believing they were serious, demanded to know how Cath could tell it was a sweet mouse and not an evil one. When I suggested that the mouse might, after all, rather like its current home, the conversation grew heated. Deborah ascended the stairs two at a time and quickly allied herself with Cath and Heather: any feminism worth its salt couldn't just be about humans. In the new world we were creating, women must model responsible behavior towards the whole living planet. And so Cath set off to drive the mouse several miles north to a pleasant-looking patch of green where the confused creature would presumably scurry away to join a new household.

"While everyone's here . . ." Deborah said. We all paused near the door. I was longing for my bacon sandwich. "What are we going to do about the blocked drains?"

Whenever the coin-collecting man from the telephone company was waiting on the doorstep or someone's sister called asking to stay overnight with her fifteen-year-old son, our no-men-in-the-house policy threw us into a quandary. Now we needed the drains fixed and nobody knew of a woman plumber. Euni remarked that we wouldn't actually have to converse with the plumber and Deborah threw up her hands, but in the end all we could do was agree, grudgingly, to let the man in and keep an eye on him.

BONE-COLD NIGHTS gave way to plain old English damp as for-sythia flaunted a brilliant yellow spring and I continued to be bowled along by the gusty breezes of change. We were building a feminist universe whose boundaries were not yet pressing in on me as later they would. Probably we all glanced at the headlines as we walked past newsstands—Margaret Thatcher had just been elected leader of the Tories though no one at Elgin was much interested in that kind of news. The internet was still more than two decades away, cell phones unheard of, and long-distance calls expensive, but we had our own net-works, mainly the passing of information from one woman to another at meetings—not very different, really, from the centuries-old trading of news at the village well. For books and pamphlets, we relied on slow mail from the States, passing them around until hundreds of women had read them. When the binding glue gave out, wads of pages fell behind our sofa cushions to rest with lost pennies, a frayed sock, and Mars bar wrappers, waiting to be chewed up by the mice.

We were not the only feminist squatters in London. One of the more notorious groups had taken over a large house in an upscale part of St John's Wood, not a usual neighborhood for a squat. The boarded-up front door, the distinctly dykey appearance of the women who moved in there, and their weekly ritual of heating bathwater over a fire in the back garden since they had no electricity, soon made them the talk of the street.

A few of them, two or three at a time, had tried out the local pub, which offered good, cheap food and, one Sunday, Cath joined the scruffy bunch that trooped in to claim a table for lunch. One and then another went up to the bar to place the orders, but each time the landlord ignored them. When nobody got a menu or an explanation as to why, they got pretty steamed up. Since the Sex Discrimination Act was about to be read again in Parliament, it occurred to one of them to phone a friend who was a reporter.

Firmly refusing to leave until they were served, they lingered on at their table after the bell for last orders rang. It must have been the landlord who called the police, for within minutes of the bell the cops arrived and started dragging them outside. When they resisted, the policemen pushed them into the gutter, holding them down with their knees, beating them with truncheons, and banging some of them hard against the wall. A few women were momentarily knocked out. All were badly bruised before being taken away and charged with crimes including Actual Bodily Harm, Assault, and Obstructing a Policeman in the Course of his Duty. Cath, who they claimed had pulled the buttons off a policeman's raincoat as she fell into the gutter, was charged with Malicious Damage to Police Property and described in newspaper reports as "the lady doctor who attacked a policeman."

When the day of their trial came around, I fell in with the large crowd that surged into the courtroom. Settling onto a hard wooden bench, I added my rumbles of disapproval when a cop lied on the stand and joined in with the burst of derisive laughter that greeted the publican when he appeared with his arm in a sling. I seethed with indignation at the blatant unfairness, although at the same time there was something empowering about our shared outrage. While the defendants munched on crisps and napped, their woman lawyer argued that the landlord and the police had acted out of prejudice. The obvious word to describe the women in the dock remained unspoken.

They were found guilty of all charges, though no one went to jail. Much later, in the High Court, they unsuccessfully sued *The Daily Express* for libel because of a double page article it published under the headline "Animal Girl Invasion." Cath, our gentle champion of the mouse, could well have been described as an animal girl—but that wasn't what they meant.

NONE OF us lived completely in the world we were creating. I rushed out to classes several times a week at the decidedly unfeminist Northeast London Poly, where I had signed up on a whim to try for a psychology degree. There I met with my male advisor who was remarkably tolerant of my feminist rants. I also remained in erratic contact with my family, though the minute I walked into my brother's house the familiar dread of discovery, the long-ingrained habits of the closet, were reawakened. The only difference was that now it took much more energy to lie: whipping out an alternate life no longer came automatically. If I'd only known how, I would gladly have given up all the pretense.

At night, under my mother's old Swedish blanket, I had one vivid dream that recurred with minor variations.

"Listen, Ma," I say in the dream, "I need to talk to you." She is folding laundry or she is vacuuming. Whatever she is doing, I will be interrupting her.

"Listen, Ma," I say again.

This time she's stacking the dishwasher, taking out the plates my father has put in the wrong place; or maybe chopping raw meat on a wooden board for the dachshunds' dinner; the dogs sit at her feet, inhaling.

I know in the dream that she'll listen to my lesbian confession and then she'll say, "but don't tell your father. It will kill him." I dream-laugh uproariously because it can't kill him now; he's already dead.

One night she's playing the piano, sight-reading the accompaniment to my clarinet sonata. Later she frowns over her glasses and, putting the music aside, picks up her crossword.

"Come on Ma, I've got one for you: three-syllable word beginning with *l*. The clue is your daughter. Got it?"

"Hmmm. Long-legged?"

"Nope."

"Lachrymose?"

"No."

"Leprechaun?"

"No, Ma. Don't be silly."

She looks up from her rolltop desk, where now she's writing to Aunt Joan.

"Well, how many letters, then?"

"Seven.

The last time I have this dream, she is lying down elevating her varicose veins.

"Is the word ladylike?" she asks. Oh no—that has eight letters. Liberal, maybe?"

"No, no, and anyway I'm not ladylike. I'm not what you think I am. Don't you get it?"

"Yes," she sighs. "I got it a long time ago. But the word I choose also has seven letters and three syllables. It's 'likable.'"

Enormous relief washes over me. I grab the bedclothes and turn over, my blood pulsing iambically: *my mother knows, my mother knows*, but the joyful beats slowly fall out of their rhythm into a stammer. Would she have offered that "likable" if she were still alive?

IN MY room by the front door I fell asleep only when the last woman came home, and woke up when the first went out in the morning. I was also roused by the alarm clock ringing in the next-door house, which shared the east wall of my room, or by the school's early band practice in the playground. Ignoring exhaustion, I spent hours at the typewriter, drafting and revising the poems I would take to the Literature Collective where we marveled at each other's brilliance (the concept of critique hadn't yet struck us as useful).

Staring at the plum-colored wall, I bashed the keys of the Remington. My table was the only thing I kept tidy with its piles of paper next to six or seven copies of *Spare Rib*—the yellow issue with my name right there on the front cover and my first published poems inside.

I started keeping drafts of my poems in a mottled grey, utilitarian box file I'd found in the bottom drawer of Ma's rolltop desk after she died. It looked like something you'd use to store bills, but the three books on writing fiction and unopened ream of paper in that same drawer hinted that she'd been planning to keep her own stories in it— not that I'd ever known her to consider becoming a writer. I couldn't bear its emptiness, its spring clip holding down nothing, so I started to fill it with my own work.

WESTERING

IN THE summer of 1975 Lilian, my on-again, off-again lover, was making one of her regular trips to visit her mother in New York. I was surprised when she invited me to go with her to spend a few days together in the city, leaving me a few weeks to explore on my own before meeting up for a camping trip in the Berkshires. It would be my first time in the States. My only reluctance was the flying as I suffered from plane phobia, but I found a special deal offering a trip over by sea on the QE2 with a return by air. At least I wouldn't have to fly both ways.

When I told my housemates at Elgin Avenue about my planned sea journey, they worried that I was engaged in a psychic struggle with hostile waters, testing myself by facing down what my parents had faced with such disastrous results.

"Do you really think you should travel *alone?*" Deborah asked me more than once.

"Is it really *wise?*" said Eunice.

But I was merely excited at the prospect of being out there on the great ocean with time to myself after years of rackety communal living. And, after spending all my growing up years on the South Coast, I missed catching glimpses of the sea at the bottom of narrow turnings in town or from the cliff tops that overlooked the Channel.

A few of them accompanied me to Victoria Station, where an ordinary green train purred beside the platform waiting to whisk its passengers off to Southampton docks. I heaved my backpack inside, slammed the door, and leaned from a window, as characters do in films when they are going off to war or leaving a doomed affair. My little group, a bunch of short-haired women in scruffy jeans and Portobello Road waistcoats, were surrounded by men in linen jackets whose wives tapped along behind porters hauling trolleys with matching suitcases. Heather reassured me they would take good care of Sheba and warned me to watch out for gun-toting muggers. At the last minute, she stepped forward, handing up a square box. "This should make the journey more fun," she said, glancing around. "Don't open it till you're in your cabin."

After negotiating the maze of the ship's interior, careful to keep the box upright, I pushed the door open and, in my best black ankle boots, stepped over the threshold. In a burst of extravagance, I'd blown the last of my savings on a room of my own in which I planned to read Simone de Beauvoir, write a travel journal, and contemplate my chaotic life. I stashed my red backpack, which held, in the bottom pocket, six of my mother's Georgian silver spoons, wrapped in a swimsuit, to sell in case of emergency. Then I sat on the bed and opened the box to discover a gooey, lopsided chocolate cake. Lifting it to my nose, I inhaled, under the sugary fumes, the rotting scent of marijuana.

That first day at sea I slept through lunch and woke from a dream of the summer I was nine. My parents took me to a place called Westward Ho! in Devon. How enchanting—a town with a name that included punctuation! On holiday there, we stood on a cliff by a lighthouse where huge seas boiled. After sneaking a glimpse of the turmoil far below, I startled my mother by striking a pose and yelling some lines from Henry V that I'd had to memorize at school: "as fearfully as doth a gallèd rock o'erhang and jutty his confounded base, swill'd with the wild and wasteful ocean . . ."

"That's nice, dear, but I can't hear you properly," Ma had shouted, her words flung away into the maelstrom. "Tell me in the car."

Walking back to the car park across bouncy, emerald grass, the gale knocked me sideways. All the sheep stoically faced the same direction, their wool pressed flat against one side and springing away from tangled ruffs on the other. We had climbed to the top of the lighthouse, where mother touched my arm and pointed into the empty space between the whitecapped ocean and the roiling clouds. "That's the way to America," she had said matter-of-factly.

I lay on my cabin bed and, as the image of my mother faded, began to worry about dinner. The photographs in the brochure had shown men and women dressed in evening togs, the women ultrafeminine, the men suave and manly. Since I had recently exchanged my last two skirts for jeans and a charity-shop leather jacket, my best outfit consisted of a pair of black pants and a jade silk shirt, which I would wear to nearly every meal.

I ate six dinners, seven breakfasts, and five lunches at my table for eight. I can only remember Randall, the Harvard student who sat on my left and who, on that first night, announced that since the price of the ticket included all you could eat, he intended to get his money's worth. Sure enough, as the days unfolded, he devoured soups and oyster appetizers, fish courses of salmon and entrees of tender pink roast beef, piled every conceivable kind of vegetable high on his plate, and wound up cheerfully with cream-filled desserts, ripe Stilton, and fruit. Understandably, he didn't talk much.

The rest of us chatted about nothing in particular: the food, the weather, the relative merits of the ship's swimming pools, the movie selections, and the hairdressers (women) or the gyms (men). Then came more personal questions. Inevitably someone asked about my family and they all looked my way, feigning interest. "My parents are dead," I muttered ungraciously, and an awkward silence fell. Then, suspecting that it would be somewhat tactless to describe their mid-Atlantic demise, I added brightly, "my brother and sister live in the South of

England." For a long moment, I waited to be asked if I was married or engaged. Should I say I was divorced, which was true but misleading? There was no way I could mention Lilian, whom I was on my way to meet; how to define her would be only the first in a long series of problems. I was not willing to call her "my friend." Even if my delicate insinuation led them to pick up the unspoken "more than just a friend," why should I reveal an unwillingness to name her my lover? Why pander to their discomfort? Or was it really my own wretched discomfort?

On the third day, the ship met a hurricane.

A long detour added an extra day to the trip and didn't entirely bypass the towering waves of Tropical Storm Amy, which caused even the well-stabilized QE2 to shudder and roll. Passengers—hundreds of them—disappeared as if by some conjuring trick after the medical officer offered anti-seasick shots that knocked you out for hours. I was confident that I wouldn't be sick and didn't take it. Instead, I found myself in the midst of a reverse Sleeping Beauty story, a minor character left awake while almost everyone else dreamed away the days.

Our table for eight was reduced to two. The waiters wove their way on practiced legs across the tilting dining room with trays on their shoulders. Everything was anchored down. Starched napkins bloomed like double tulips out of slender glasses in front of empty seats. The creaking of something—perhaps a steel plate low on the ship's hull—was just audible whenever the ubiquitous soft music paused.

On the stormiest night, I wandered around the deserted lounges until I found a window that offered a view of the outdoors, now off-limits due to the weather. Alone with just the hum of engines, I watched curtains of spray blow across the games deck, illuminated for a moment by the flickering lamps. Beyond this square, lit area, I could see nothing, though I could imagine the raging seas. In order to skirt the hurricane, the ship had veered to the north. I thought about icebergs, the Titanic, and the power of the swells smashing into the ship's flanks.

AS THE waves subsided, the PA system started giving details of the ship's speed and progress and the betting on our arrival time in New York heated up. I began to worry about the cake, which was only half gone. The last night's dinner over, my brain addled by the two slices I'd bolted during the cocktail hour, I tried to calculate the chances of deportation if I got caught carrying it through customs. Negotiating the now-familiar passages, I descended staircases, turned corners, and trudged along more corridors, the pot stretching minutes into hours. All the cabin doors looked the same, but each one could tell a story. What story would mine tell, I thought, and chuckled out loud: there's a woman in there, adrift from her moorings. I chuckled again, a choking kind of laugh that hinted at the closeness of tears.

I pulled the cake from my miniature refrigerator and considered the options, then took my tent from its canvas bag and untied the laces of the pouch that held six hollow, aluminum tent poles. Grabbing handfuls of chocolate sponge and frosting, I stuffed the remains of the cake up inside them. Worn out, I dropped on to the bed and fell asleep among the crumbs.

At about 2 a.m., I woke up with a pounding heart. Using a curtain rod, I poked the cake out of the poles onto a newspaper. Then I stood naked in the shower and ran the hot water through the poles, folded up the newspaper with the mess of cake inside, threw on some clothes, and went upstairs. As I remember it, I skulked towards the lee-side deck rail, though that may be a bit too much like a slapstick movie to hold true. Probably I did glance around, though, before hurling the package out into the night. I clutched my thin T-shirt to my body and glanced up at the stars, all winking at me.

Later that morning, after the ship had cruised past the Statue of Liberty and moored up in the great city that looked just as it always looked in the movies, I marched into the customs shed. The officer went straight for what must be a well-known hiding place, pulled the tent poles out of their bag, and held them up to the light to examine their interiors while I tried to look casual. "Have a good stay," he said, eyeing my breasts.

The streets were littered with cans and plastic sacks disgorging stinking refuse as I hauled my pack into the sweltering heat and started to walk along what I now had to call the sidewalk. I had heard there was a garbage strike on but could never have imagined this dismal scene. Later that night, booked into a hotel with Lilian, I told her that I hated New York; when she left to visit her family, I would take the Greyhound to San Francisco.

"What the fuck do you want to do that for?" Lilian said. Our reunion had, as usual, been both ardent and anxious—the ardor easily ignited, the anxiety rooted in familiar suspicion. We were both fishing for clues that might extinguish or fan the flames of jealousy.

Greyhound buses had been marketed in England as a cool, even glamorous, way for young adventurers to travel in the US and I'd seen photos of San Francisco's gay pride parade. My blood and bones knew that it was the place all lesbian roads led to. Even before Harvey Milk and the murders, before the demonstrations and the ballot initiatives, just about every gay person in the world knew that city was our Mecca.

I boarded the bus wearing a pair of washed-out jeans, onto which I had sewn an array of colorful patches. My denim jacket was darker blue, and soon I acquired a red cowboy bandanna, which I knotted around my neck to make me look jaunty. It didn't take long to discover that the buses bore little resemblance to the color images I'd seen in the Sunday papers in which a coach full of merry folk swooped through the Rockies or rolled across the prairies; mine was grubby with soiled upholstery, an odor of diesel, and a truly repellent onboard lavatory.

In Pittsburgh I slept on the floor of the sister of someone I knew in London. There were other footloose women staying there and the next morning two of them offered me a ride in their Volkswagen camper to a radical faerie commune in Arkansas. I accepted happily, though I had no idea what a faerie was let alone where Arkansas was.

I'd been calling Lilian frequently from phone boxes in bus stations. Now I called her again and left a message at her mother's apartment.

"I'm off to Arkansas with two dykes in a camper," I said, enjoying the message as much for the picture it painted of me as for the fleeting connection with Lilian. But that would be the last call I made for some time. Although the two women were lovers, and had been for what then seemed like a long time (a year, perhaps), nevertheless, Trish, the tall one with a mane of tangled blonde hair, contrived to sit in the middle of the bench seat as we trundled south on roads that were called parkways or interstates. As we grew sleepy, Trish's head fell onto my shoulder and her hand landed on my thigh.

Late that night, after a barbecue with forty or fifty gay men, most wearing skirts or tiny tight shorts, and a few prancing in tiaras, I sat around the campfire and tried to think of things to say. There was a nocturnal din made by tree frogs or crickets—I recognized no American wildlife at this point—and the humidity had a friendly touch. Light from the fire flickered across their eager, sunburnt faces as they eyed one another and grilled me about the gay male scene "across the pond." All I could think to tell them was the story of going to Bethnal Rouge, a gay commune in Bethnal Green, in search of a husband for my American friend Sheila, so she could stay in London. The guy who volunteered, introduced only as Nigel, showed up dutifully at the registry office and said his "I do." When he signed the book "Nigel Dalloway" we all let out a hoot of delight. Sheila, whose PhD thesis was on Woolf, had become Mrs. Dalloway.

After midnight, groggy from cheap red wine, I stumbled to a shed I'd been allocated and fell asleep on a bench. Sometime later, I half woke up to find Trish kissing her way into my old, green sleeping bag. As usual, my first response, after the onset of sexual interest, was remorse.

"Get out of here," I whispered, feeling both virtuous and ambivalent, and Trish did, after a few minutes' whispered pleading, disappear into the spangled night. In the morning, both she and her lover were grouchy. They were staying on with the faeries but gave me a ride to the nearest bus station.

After that, calling Lilian felt too dangerous. Nocturnal encounters weren't something I could include in the story I was relaying back to New York, and Lilian had always had an uncanny knack of knowing when I was leaving things out. If she even suspected something like this, she would weep and throw out accusations—usually correct—about my untrustworthiness.

"You don't love me at all," she had sobbed so many times.

Knowing of love only the desperate urge to kiss and be kissed, and of course everything that kissing led to, I would answer routinely, "Of course I do."

I WOKE up at dawn somewhere in the middle of Oklahoma. The sun, not yet above the horizon, was announcing itself with a wash of gold. My forehead, pressed against the window of the bus, ached. As I opened my eyes, all I could see were the colors of emptiness—the land, infinite and bare, stretching away in shades of ochre; the sky, bigger than I had ever known it, streaked with wispy clouds whose edges gleamed. I straightened up, dread rising in my throat, and looked ahead through the windshield. The highway ran on forever in a straight line. Turning back to my window, I expected to see at least a few farms or fences, a lonely shack or a corral, but was confronted instead with a mirror image of the view on the other side. With mounting horror, I looked back towards New York; perhaps we had passed through some small town that I would now see receding into the distance. But there was nothing.

In my early twenties I'd been either adventurous or foolhardy, depending on how you look at it, when I had driven alone all over Europe, crossed Alpine passes in storms, and found my way at night through Spanish mountains populated by bandits. Here, though, was a landscape far more dangerous. I might step down from the bus and walk away with nothing but my shadow between me and the sadness I'd kept at bay for so long. Like one of those tumbleweeds, sorrow would bounce all the way to the horizon and when it returned it would, for sure, knock me for six. I grabbed the arms of my seat.

Should I take the next Greyhound back to New York or go on to the West Coast? On my tattered map I traced my route: it would be as far to go back as it would be to go on. My finger landed on the red dot that was San Francisco.

People got on and off the bus. Some chattered nonstop; others fell immediately asleep, their chins resting on their chests, and nodded down until they fell forward and woke with a snort or a mumbled apology. Only three or four of us were going all the way, muttering "hi" to one another as we climbed back on board after each stop, and occasionally exchanging wrinkled paperbacks. Once, I looked up from Marge Piercy's *Woman on the Edge of Time* as a greasy-haired man in a blue suit and orange socks slid into the seat next to me. I pretended to sleep, but every time I stirred or recrossed my legs, he jerked to attention with: "You travelin' all alone, darlin?" Eventually we reached a rest stop where I was relieved to see the guy stride out to the highway and climb into a waiting pickup truck. Bus-weary, eating a ham and cheese on a wooden bench with a view of two trailers and an assortment of dogs lying among the flies, I consulted my map again and decided to leave the bus for at least one night in Albuquerque, a place whose name I had no idea how to pronounce. I would find my way to a lesbian bar if there was one to find.

I had been told that was the place to go to meet lesbians. The only lesbian bar in London, as far as I knew, was the Gateways, a bastion of old-time closeted dykes since 1930. No self-respecting feminist would go there: when we wanted to dance, we went to discos—clubs or pubs that dedicated one night a week to women. More than once, I'd been at a club on Oxford Street when it was raided by the police, and on another wild night I'd run from the disco at the Crown and Woolpack when a knife fight broke out between ex-lovers.

The women I stopped for directions that evening had a particular air about them that I recognized: part exhilaration, part hopefulness, and part bravado. They invited me to stay at their house, though it turned out not to be theirs but Meg's; they were simply crashing there. In the bar they led me to, I was enchanted with the jukebox that flashed colored lights and gulped quarters with a metallic clunk, just like the one on *Happy Days* where the cool Fonz, with his greased-back hair, liked to slouch. When my guides disappeared into the crowd, the jukebox became a useful prop against which I could lean and survey the scene as if contemplating which song to choose, rather than hoping I'd find someone to dance with. I eyed a woman who looked both trendy and casual in her shorts and tangerine T-shirt. She was sitting on a bar stool and had kicked off her sandals, her tanned, bare feet curling over a rung. Catching my glance, she jerked her head slightly towards the dance floor and slid from her perch. I sauntered over to her as the jukebox began to ask, "*Voulez-vous coucher avec moi ce soir?*" An hour later we were slow dancing in a corner to "The First Time Ever I Saw Your Face," and I was refusing to think about how Lilian always cried to Roberta Flack.

At breakfast, I met my hostess, who taught in the women's studies department at the university. I fell for her sultry voice and untamed laugh and managed to spend at least part of three nights in her bed, though she kicked me out in the early hours to prevent her two children from finding out what she was up to. The sense of wrongdoing that had prevented me from picking up the telephone along the way escalated; by now Lilian must surely know something was up. When I did finally talk to her, I'd be thoroughly interrogated and my throbbing conscience would wing its way back across all that empty space. Still, I agreed to Meg's suggestion that we should meet in ten days' time for some camping in the Rockies.

Back on the bus I traversed a sizzling Arizona. Every once in a while, I pulled out the map and inked over an inch or two of Route 66. At some point, as sweat began to stain the back of my seat, I realized that even Arizona in a heat wave couldn't account for my flushed face and throbbing head. Seeing me at a rest stop holding my forehead, a woman with two little girls in pink shorts asked me if I was all right and, when I ventured that perhaps I was a bit sick, offered what looked like a fairly clean thermometer. 103 degrees. I stocked up on bottles of juice and aspirin and climbed the steps once again.

My bus dreams grew all mixed up. Lilian waved a pamphlet. Meg crooned in the seat behind me. A lurid jukebox pulsed in time with my blood. I dreamed I was six again, in the safe cocoon of my parents' car; in the back seat I was a sleeping child, waking and sleeping while someone's competent hands on the wheel swept us around curves and someone's careful foot on the pedal urged us up hills and down the other side. A groan escaped from my throat and I wiped the sweat off my face with my no-longer-jaunty bandanna. Then, two boys with guitars started strumming on the back seat, "Hey! Mister Tambourine Man . . ." Much later, one of them yelled, "Hey man, we're in California!"

San Francisco was breezy, the bridge and the summer grasses were golden, and my friend Shay from London had become a Californian in a cowboy hat, working at a riding school. Buoyant again, I climbed the steep streets between multicolored houses and thought of being, very soon, in the Rockies with Meg. It was at Shay's riding stable, using the wall phone and inhaling the scent of horse manure, that I finally gritted my teeth and called Lilian. She picked up almost before the first ring and greeted me with "Where the fuck have you been?" So I had to confess—sort of—that on my way back east, before I met up with her again, I would be going camping with a woman who had, at least temporarily, beguiled me.

The trip Lilian and I had planned in the Berkshires was now destined to be full of familiar *Sturm und Drang* and sure enough, when we found a campsite near enough to Tanglewood to catch a concert, Lilian interrupted the string quartet by periodically hissing in my ear that I had criminally deserted her. I cringed apologetically for two days and nights until she finally confessed to having picked up a "cute lesbian" in a Provincetown bar and spent two nights with her while I'd been camping in the Rockies with Meg.

Lilian and I squirmed in the tight embrace of my tent and, no matter how high we hoisted our food bag on its line between the trees, the raccoons got into it. We were committed as ever to forging some new kind of relationship that remained vague and undefined: like an ambitious cocktail full of new ingredients, we'd shaken and stirred ourselves over and over again until nothing tasted familiar, nothing flowed as we expected—except, of course, our periods. Our blood, answering to some mysterious connection between us, paid no attention to who was right or wrong or whether we happened to be loving or hating each other that month. Its synchronized dripping, its gushing, its scarlet clotting, promised a harmony we never managed to achieve.

While we bickered in a desultory way there in the Berkshires, I reverted to daydreams about the capacious tent Meg and I had shared in Colorado, where her long hair fell around me, making its own tent for our two faces. It was there, while the aspens sighed their long sighs, that I'd promised I would return to America the following summer.

BACK IN England, Lilian and I spent much of our time breaking up, rethinking the breakup, and then breaking up again. Although I felt trapped when we were together and anxious when we separated, most of my emotional energy stayed focused on Meg, who wrote me long letters and mailed me audio tapes that featured lyrical memories of our camping trip and a lot of heavy breathing. I had said I would spend the summer of '76 back in the States with her, and nothing was going to stop me. On the day of my departure Lilian stepped into the street to watch my taxi disappear down Ladbroke Grove and yelled after me, "You think you're leaving but you'll be back"—more of a threat than a reassurance.

By this time, Meg had been hired as the coordinator of women's studies at Portland State and moved to Oregon, a place I had never heard of. I flew to Seattle where I already had a ticket for the short hop down to Portland, but my plane phobia kicked in and I spent a ridiculous amount of money on an assortment of shuttles and buses, began a short-lived love affair with BLT sandwiches, and eventually arrived at the Portland bus station, where Meg and her two children bundled me into her candy-wrapper-filled station wagon.

It took only a few weeks for Meg's demanding job, her jealous children, and a coterie of possessive admirers to freeze me out of my romantic aspirations. But even while I was contemplating moving out of her house, I was becoming intrigued with Portland which, at that time, had a greater percentage of lesbians per capita than any city in the United States. There was a feminist bookstore, a café, a credit union, law collective, dinner collectives, and clothing exchange parties. There were even all-women construction companies. There were groups of women who worked on abortion rights, violence against women, and childcare. What with lesbian bars and women-only concerts and softball teams, it was almost possible to live in an entirely female world. Its playful energy was punctuated only occasionally by simmering resentments and unacknowledged grievances. But no matter what differences arose, we all spun inside our world together, as if at the funfair, whirling faster and faster in that circular room where the floor falls away, leaving everyone plastered flat against the wall.

My accent drew women to me: dykes in tight T-shirts at the Rising Moon asked me to repeat ordinary figures of speech; women whose jeans stretched across their buttocks lined up to teach me to play pool. Taking advantage of this, I fell into one-night stands or two-week flings. Then, for a while, I tried to settle down and live with Harriet, a woman I had just met, and her two girls, but parenting and growing vegetables didn't come easily to me.

This women's community was utterly different from the permanently high-pitched factions in England, and I reveled in its strangeness just as I had once reveled in the foreignness of Spain, where I'd lived in a whirl of sensation that masked loneliness. At the end of the summer, my friends from London, Heather and Eunice, arrived in

Portland to pick me up for a long-planned trip to Mexico, but I was in a settled-down phase with Harriet and stayed behind. Before they left, the three of us took a tent and hiked around Mount Hood for a few days, ineptly blistering our feet and running out of food, surrounded by red huckleberries we didn't know were edible.

I patched together a measly income from housecleaning, which was a fair disaster as I never saw the point of cleaning underneath things: chairs and beds hid their private stores of dust balls, toasters squatted on layers of crumbs, and rugs spilled lint and cat hair from their edges. When nobody was home at the *Sunset Magazine* houses I was supposed to be tending, I would sprawl in a comfortable armchair, jotting poetic phrases in the journal I was required to keep for a writing class I'd signed up for. When the weather grew hot, I threw off my clothes and dived into the swimming pool where, sooner or later, I was discovered, naked, by a husband coming home unexpectedly. My shortcomings as a cleaner now revealed, I moved on to the more demanding and sometimes frightening job of cleaning offices and warehouses at night.

The excitement of exploring Portland's lesbian life began to wear off, and homesickness set in. I found myself missing the panoply of greens I'd grown up with; I missed polite reticence and averted eyes; I even missed food swimming in gravy or custard. People stood so close when they talked to me that I felt like a deer cornered by a pack of baying dogs and I could never figure out how I could get them to back off. No doubt I would eventually have moved back to England, had I not fallen in love with Ruth.

BEDS

FOR A while I had been noticing Ruth: at a Holly Near concert, in the women's bookstore, even once at a dance party at her house, though I'd hardly said two words to her on that occasion. I'd begun to look around for her on Wednesday evenings, the women-only nights at Mountain Moving Cafe, and gradually my antenna for her presence in a room acquired a razor-sharp focus. I zeroed in on her as the light caught the studious, frameless glasses that dominated her small face. Her short, dark hair was already streaked with silver, creating the stunning look that often accompanies a youthful, prematurely gray contrast. Her Levi's, faded and well-worn, fit casually on her small-boned frame; yet an air of quiet confidence lent her a sense of much larger stature.

We were thrown together during a very public battle over hiring the new director of women's studies at Portland State, where I was teaching. After a national search, our committee chose Ruth for the job and the appointment was approved by deans all the way up the line until the president nixed it, never explaining why. *The Oregonian* did not use the word "lesbian" (it was on a list of words considered inappropriate to print in our major daily) although it was generally thought that this was the reason: not simply being a lesbian—there were obviously many working at the university—but being an out lesbian.

Another explanation was that her public interest law firm had represented a group of students against the university and the president had been subpoenaed. Other possibilities included her key role in negotiating the first part-time teachers union contract, or being on the legal team that got an acquittal for hundreds of protesters arrested at the Trojan Nuclear Power Plant, covered by all the national TV networks.

Polite delegations of faculty met with the president and groups of students drew up petitions; even state legislators and city counselors got involved, a huge effort that did not, in the end, succeed. In the midst of all this uproar, I met her a few times at Wilde Oscar's, a smoky gay bar downtown, to fill her in on the latest developments. We began to linger later and later, eyeing each other across a sticky table until one night we stayed so late that they started vacuuming as we slow danced in the semidark.

I had so often fallen into relationships. This time, I knew I couldn't just tumble into it—that Ruth wasn't the kind of woman who allowed things to happen haphazardly in her life, or at least that's how I saw her. One day I found an excuse to drop off something at her house, after which I lingered as long as feasible before she dashed off to something or other, escorting me out the door on her way. As soon as I started my car, I realized I had left my sunglasses in her living room. Later, when I knew she'd be home, I stopped by to pick them up and, as she handed them to me, I found myself giving her an intensely serious look followed by an almost unbearably titillating hug. As we stepped, breathless, out of each other's arms I think we both knew that we'd taken a step towards something that was bound to involve, at the very least, a wild affair; I felt scared in a way I never had before when approaching romance. This was the first time I had consciously chosen to pursue a lover—and a lover I wasn't at all sure I could hold on to.

In those days, decades before a legal partnership, not to mention actual marriage, was even imagined, we had plenty of ways to choose an anniversary: it could be marked from the first real date, first kiss, first sex, or, for some, the date of moving in together. Ruth and I have always celebrated July 9, which was in every sense the hottest day of the summer of 1979. Since we were each living with a lover, we had nowhere to go to be alone with our rapidly escalating passion, so on that sweltering day we met at the apartment of a mutual friend who had gone away, generously leaving me her keys. I unlocked the stuffy apartment, opened the windows, and found some glasses suitable for the shots of whisky that gave us the courage to throw off our clothes and fall onto the bed and each other, our skins slippery, reveling in the heat we brewed up together.

When I try to picture the rest of that summer, it's hard to peel away the golden light that suffuses every image: two women lying side by side on the slope of Laurelhurst Park, dogs panting beside them as hands slide together and heartbeats race to a frenzy inside their apparently relaxed, almost-sleeping bodies; or two women pulling up in separate cars outside a house with prayer flags strung across the yard, one fumbling with a key, the other running fingers up her lover's spine and settling them around the back of her neck as the door swings open and they step into a dim hallway.

We spend sweaty afternoons together in borrowed apartments, cooling each other off with wet facecloths and then wandering out into the bright sunlight, trying to remember if the cat should stay in or out, or where to leave the key. Sometimes we manage to spend a whole weekend together, backpacking up the north side of Mount Adams with our dogs to where the wildflowers make an impressionist painting of the high meadows, the sunsets last for hours, and we can see all the way to Mount Rainier.

Sometimes we go to Cannon Beach and stay at the Wayfarer, a funky, hippy sort of place with threadbare sheets and sagging furniture. On these trips, even in the middle of winter, no matter where we are, the sun always shines; we almost believe that our desire has the power to direct the weather.

Since we have pledged ourselves to honesty, we are open about our affair with our respective lovers, guaranteeing that the ungluing will be as messy and painful as our coming together is enthralling. When I finally tell Harriet I am moving out, she throws a pot of warm spaghetti at my head, and I can hardly blame her.

DESPITE OUR numbers, we Portland dykes were mostly invisible except to one another; even though a decade had passed since Stonewall, not a lot had changed. No woman who was known to be a lesbian had been awarded child custody in Oregon (Ruth would be the lawyer for the first successful case). Although five years earlier, the American Psychiatric Association had removed homosexuality from its list of mental disorders, it was still in a category called "sexual orientation disturbance." Gay men were beaten up outside gay bars with relative impunity because they were reluctant to involve the police, and bumper stickers like "Kill a Queer for Christ" had started to appear. "Tolerance" was the gold standard. Ruth and I hated that word and recoiled against being tolerated as if we were unruly children or mosquitoes, but truthfully, I'd have to say that in most situations it was all we hoped for.

Being hated gnawed at us, but we were not alone; we were part of a community, not just locally but nationally and to some degree internationally, trying to reimagine how to live and love without reference to heterosexuality or the prefeminist lesbians we thought—mistakenly as it turned out—had simply been aping straight couples. With supreme, unfounded confidence, we believed we could make it up as we went along with no role models. Apprentices without mentors, our most meaningful contact was with other lesbians who were as determined as we were—and just as clueless.

Ruth and I kept our separate apartments, which was rare among the dykes we knew, and did not move in together for nine years—an unheard-of length of time when it was common to move in together on the second date. We hoped that it would allow us the breathing room we needed to remain two separate people, to say nothing of avoiding the tensions of dealing with mundane life—dishes, laundry, toothpaste. More crucially, living separately allowed us each a place to retreat to when we found ourselves veering between wild infatuation and hardly being able to stand one other. We were extravagant in everything: our love, our arguments, our confidence that nothing could be more perfect or our belief that it was likely a big mistake.

Sometimes it seemed as if falling in love had pushed me right over some crazy edge. Back in the days of Nicolette, and even of Lilian, I'd had no vision of a life with a woman, even while I flailed around desperately trying to create one. In those days, I could say that I wanted to stay with my lover forever, but I could no more picture it than I'd been able to picture married life with Colin. Now it was different. I had real, tantalizing glimpses of a life with Ruth.

Having each watched from a front row seat as the other left her lover, we had built into our early years a troublesome chunk of insecurity; there's something about seeing the object of your desire abandon another that endures, aching like a phantom limb. We were plagued by late-night phone marathons, and jittery fears that we would never settle into something we could trust; intensity tore into us with unanticipated pain almost as often as it shocked us with joy. When we were in sync, I hummed through the days, full of energy and optimism, but when, seemingly out of the blue, we ran into each other's jagged edges, I panicked: I couldn't afford to mess up what felt like the best thing that had ever happened. It called for a new kind of courage—a slowly-developing muscle that was strong enough to bear the weight of trying again and again.

I could also become unhinged by ordinary separations, especially if I was the one staying home. I once pleaded with Ruth not to go to a law conference halfway across the country. The more I pleaded, the angrier she got. "Get a grip!" she said, followed by soothing reassurances that there was nothing to worry about—millions of people flew safely every day. But nothing could calm my worry as I drove her to the airport and, refusing to leave her at the door, parked and walked her in. I followed her to the gate, becoming more and more distraught. Finally, Ruth got stern and told me in a low voice to go home, but as she walked towards the door to board the plane, I grabbed her, sobbing. "If you must go," I hiccupped, "I'm coming too. We'll die together." Ruth twisted out of my clutch and ran down the jetway. I was left there, gradually emerging from the scene I'd created, a classic silent movie in which someone dashes around at triple speed waving their arms histrionically while the audience watches in horror.

It was pure craziness, of course, yet I knew something that those gawkers didn't know: someone you love can leave and never return, can be swallowed up at any time—as my parents had been—with no advance warning. Probably most people do know this but they are able to keep the knowledge behind a curtain at a safe distance; it would be years before I could do that myself. Even now I am sometimes pricked by the old fear of sudden disaster.

Occasionally, Ruth and I refer to that airport scene, the nadir of our tempestuous period, and wonder how we survived it. If you had asked her during those first few years why she didn't give up on me, she would have said without missing a beat that she knew it wouldn't last—and she meant the relationship, not the craziness. Had you asked me, though, I would have said with equal confidence that it most certainly would last; I was staking everything on it.

WHEN, IN our second year together, her mother died after a long illness, Ruth struggled to make room for grief while working long hours to meet a deadline for a brief in the Oregon Supreme Court. She, along with a lawyer for the ACLU, had brought a suit, which they argued and won later that year, requiring abortions under the state Medicaid program. I could see what I needed to do—what in fact I wanted to do for her—but I alternated between trying to be supportive and resenting the emotional burdens that felt overwhelming. The truth was that I had a limited amount of attention for anyone else's losses, having hauled around my own bundle of unacknowledged sorrow for so long. I was ashamed that my own mother's death was trying to claim my attention, butting in on the space that should have been Ruth's, even while holding her in my arms just the way I still needed someone to hold me.

Ruth was showing me how death could be mourned; her family followed the Jewish custom of sitting shiva, a week with family and friends doing nothing but talking and thinking about her mother's life and telling stories, with food brought for all of them. This was followed by a month of going back to real life but without movies, parties, etc., just the essentials. After that they honored the requirement to go back to full life, while the reality of death gradually took hold. They gathered again when the chiseled stone was placed on the grave at eleven months, another milestone in grief's journey. I envied her the comfort of these prescribed steps, shared with her community.

While Ruth's mother had been alive her father had found a way to appear accepting of us, but now his refusal to treat us the same as her partnered siblings was becoming another source of distress and her estrangement from him gradually solidified. My family too, even from far away, managed to convey disapproval on the rare occasions I spoke to them by telephone. Ruth and I sometimes joked that we were orphans—not a word often used to describe anyone in their mid-thirties, but we *felt* orphaned. Birthdays and holidays, illnesses and important decisions—all were shared with close friends rather than with our families. Years later, we would reconnect with our siblings, but we couldn't have foreseen that.

Nevertheless, we stuck with what seemed like an endless process of coming out and then coming out some more. It wasn't just a matter of taking a deep breath and leaping, but more like treading carefully across an Oregon creek whose stepping stones were slick and barely big enough to support a boot. Dangerous and thrilling at the same time, it was like learning some extreme sport with obstacles that loom up unexpectedly. Some days, strong currents threatened to pull us off balance; other days a stepping stone wobbled precariously underfoot; yet the occasions on which someone else made the passage feel safer were particularly sweet.

At Ruth's sister's wedding the usual photos were taken, starting with the bride and groom and gradually expanding to embrace more and more family. When the photographer called out, "Bride's family including in-laws," Ruth and I looked at each other. Did that mean *me*? For a long moment we hesitated there in the sunshine next to the *chuppa* in the middle of an Oregon vineyard, and then Ruth's Aunt Gail stepped behind us and gave me a friendly shove. "Out-laws too," she said.

With my family, it was a slow process. Sitting with my sister-in-law in a café on a stormy Normandy beach in 1999, so much time had passed that it seemed possible to try for a more real conversation than was the family custom. The wind was blowing sand against the flimsy building where we were drinking hot chocolate when I managed to work the word *lesbian* into our talk, and she, awkwardly and a touch defiantly, said that she'd never understood why I'd had to be so "public" about my lesbianism. "Your brother and I," she said, firmly putting an end to the topic, "never felt it necessary to broadcast our private life." The iron chair dug into my seat bones and gusts shook the walls of the lean-to. I was speechless. I thought about how she daily breathed the air of acceptance and approval: her wedding, the births of her children, the family life she lived in full view of friends and neighbors.

RUTH LEFT the feminist law collective she had helped found and took a job as a litigation coordinator for the statewide legal services program where, unsurprisingly, all the other lawyers were men and all the support staff women. From the beginning, we were known as a couple there, and Ruth was liked and respected until the day she discovered that the unmarried girlfriends of her male colleagues had been provided with health insurance. When she asked the director to include me, he refused. Her employment contract said they couldn't discriminate on the basis of "sexual preference," so rather than extend coverage to me, he dug in and took it away from the others—a move deliberately designed to punish her for refusing to back down.

Being an out lesbian, perhaps surprisingly, was not always easy even in women's studies programs; I had been shocked and hurt by homophobic hostility. At some point in those early years together, we each said we'd had enough and left our jobs. Neither of us would ever be an employee again. We worked on contract or for ourselves, always on our own terms. Ruth taught a sex discrimination seminar at the law school; I taught writing classes and wrote op-eds that I syndicated to papers around the country. We had hardly any money but we didn't care. We read and reread every important feminist writer of that era and felt buoyed by the energy of our movement, savoring every gain. Feminism and our friends, in addition to our love for one another, were what mattered.

Caught up in what was known then as the Women in Print Movement, Ruth started a feminist press, The Eighth Mountain— named for her mother whose birth name was Achtenberg—and began to publish literature by women. Together we created The Flight of the Mind (named after Virginia Woolf, who used the phrase to describe her joy in pursuing words), a summer writing workshop program for women on the McKenzie River, which ran for eighteen years, and later, with several others, Soapstone, a retreat for women writers in the Oregon Coast Range. But all that was in the future.

I WAS always eager for us to get away, whether just to the beach or across the Atlantic. No doubt because I had come of age before feminism and had to conduct love affairs in secret, "going away"—almost anywhere—held an allure. Back then it meant freedom from discovery and from having to make up lies. Although Ruth and I were not trying to hide, I still thought of a trip as a magic interlude. In fact, for us, traveling usually did mean long spells of peaceful togetherness. But, of course, there was nowhere we could go that didn't require some degree of deception.

"Do you have a room for two available?" I asked in my best French. It could have been anywhere, but it was actually Cahors. We were on holiday, driving south from England through France and Spain in 1981.

The woman behind the desk looked at me over half-glasses, her penciled eyebrows raised, and assessed me for a moment. I watched as she lost interest: it was always the same—quite ordinary, at least for most guests. But not for me. I knew the dreaded question was about to emerge from the woman's immaculately painted, French lips—the question that was so simple, so complicated, so well designed to make me feel wrong from head to toe. And it's easy to feel that way in France.

I turned away and stared at the yellow orchid at the end of the counter. Russet-colored stripes marked the pathway into the throat of the flower, nature's runway for whatever insect it was that ventured in there to pollinate—a simple guide to something necessary and natural. Just what I needed now as the question moved through the woman's mouth, passed between her even, nicotine-stained teeth, and landed between us in the air above the counter:

"A room with two single beds or a double, madame?" Only in French she called the double bed *un lit matrimonial.*

It wasn't long after this (I had failed to muster the courage to ask for the matrimonial bed) that I refused to be the hotel negotiator any longer.

I was the driver; Ruth with her marginal grasp of romance languages would have to be the one to go in and ask for the bed that's made for those who are matrimonially related—or who can pass as such. Until then I had assumed that I had to be both driver and room-getter.

"From now on," I said, "I will be the big surprise who walks in after the deal is done."

I preferred this role. In spite of my burgeoning success in the truth-telling arena, I liked to pretend I had nothing to do with choosing our bed. I could even tell myself that it hadn't been chosen at all: for all I knew it was the only room left—the only bed available for hundreds of miles. I could heave the baggage up seven flights of stairs with goodwill (even though I wasn't a matrimonial person) and my dignity, at the top of the stairs, would remain intact.

This was very effective in Figueres, Barcelona, Gerona, and several *pueblos* further south. As Ruth disappeared into hotels while I sat in the car studying the map, I was curious about how she managed to secure the *matrimonio* for us, but didn't ask. Maybe she had resorted to the comparative pricing method, one I had used quite often before I resigned. This involved asking carefully which was the cheaper option—singles or a double. Inevitably the double was the cheapest, allowing a budget-minded traveler to sacrifice herself and sleep with her traveling companion in the interests of economy.

I had discovered this method in the mid-sixties, on my first vacation in Spain with my second lover, Jean. We'd both felt so sheepish about what we did in the *matrimonio* that we couldn't even look the receptionist in the eye. But from some stubborn core—perhaps the same one that had propelled me into the relationship in the first place—I dredged up a determination not to pay extra for two beds that slid apart in the middle of the night. In those days, I wouldn't have dreamed of handing over the job—not just because Jean didn't speak French or Spanish, but because it was my responsibility. I drove the car, made the arrangements, and took care of her. If we hadn't been in such denial, and if we had known anything at all about lesbians, which we didn't, we might have said I was stuck with being the butch.

Now I was no longer wedded (in the metaphorical, not the matrimonial, sense) to being butch. I was happy to sit and doze or to search for a parking space while Ruth did whatever it was she did to get us what we wanted.

Somewhere near Palafrugell, we stopped, exhausted, at an inn on the highway. It was dark and had turned cold; we couldn't wait to fall into bed. Eagerly we went in together and found a toothless woman sitting in front of a flickering television, knitting. Ruth asked for the room, but was ignored.

"*Tiene usted un habitación, por favor?*" I almost pleaded. The old woman glanced up briefly from the television.

"Two singles?" she said in Spanish.

I rolled my eyes at Ruth who placed a hand on my arm calmingly. "Tell her I have to have a double bed to do my back exercises on," she said.

I looked at her in disbelief. Was this what she had been telling hotel managers, receptionists, maids, and night porters up and down the length of Spain? Back exercises?

"I can't do that," I said. "She'll think we're really weird."

"Then tell her we want a double bed because we're lovers and we do unspeakable things together in bed." Stumbling, I tried to explain about the *ejercicios* for the *doloroso* back, but the crone had picked up her knitting and was absorbed in the movie again. Interrupting my blushing explanation, she yelled in that piercing voice possessed by most Spanish women: "*Jesús! Venga Jesús!*" For a moment I thought she was invoking Christ to save her from these foreigners who were either crazy (the exercises) or immoral (the conversation that she might have understood). A wizened man shuffled in and picked up the lightest of our bags, leading the way upstairs to a freezing cold room with a double bed. Jesús: the porter.

Exhaustion and cold proved too much for Ruth, who shivered all night, in spite of my three forays downstairs for extra blankets. The third time, handing me two more, Jesús muttered something about *ejercicios* keeping a person warm, so I knew we had been discussed.

On our last night in Spain, in the fishing village of Puerto de la

Selva—a place I'd known when I lived near there—we splurged for a room at the hotel right on the quayside. Its outdoor tables were bright with red check tablecloths and its indoor restaurant opened on both sides to the ocean. Ruth had dealt with the question, though unfortunately we'd ended up with two single beds anyway—perhaps because that was all they had left. Unpacking our bags in the room with a magnificent view over the clear, green water, I routinely pulled out the table from between them and put it to one side. Then we pushed them together, resigned to a night of avoiding the central chasm.

We swam off the rocks, sat at a table by the harbor wall to eat a paella, and then, in search of a few last-minute treasures, wandered arm in arm through the town. Two women holding hands was not an unusual sight in Spain; in fact, it was the custom. Sexual contact, however, had until recently been a crime—it was just six years since Franco's death—and gay men could still be thrown in jail for public displays of affection.

Lingering over a bottle of champagne, we discussed our return journey through France, determined to eke out our few remaining francs by avoiding hotels altogether and using the tent we had stashed in the trunk. The only thing that worried us was the cold: the nights were growing shorter and chillier and our aged sleeping bags were skimpy.

The noise from the bar went on till the early hours, but we slept through most of it and woke early to pack. Then we went into the dining room and sat at a table near the open doors for breakfast. We ordered coffee and stared out at the sailboats rocking on their moorings as the sun appeared over Cabo Creus and began to light up the bay. Just then, a large man dressed in black with a white apron—the man who had carried our bags the night before—walked up to our table with a strange leer on his face. He hovered for a minute, not speaking, yet not going away either, smirking as if he were possessed of some dreadful secret. Just as I was about to ask what he wanted, or summon a waiter to send him away, he lifted both arms in the air with his fists clenched and spat.

He was gone before either of us fully registered what had happened. Gone so fast and so completely that it was hard to believe he had ever been there. The coffee and croissants arrived. Peach jam and four squares of butter. I looked outside, trying to feel something. Trying to know what to feel. The sun was higher, the yachts' masts glinting and the wrought iron lamp posts on the quayside casting shadows. I poured the coffee and avoided looking at Ruth or at the people sitting nearby. For a few brief moments I hung my head and remembered what it was like to feel responsible for other people's contempt. I looked up at Ruth, who seemed bewildered and when I reached for her hand she didn't move. Then, holding her gaze with mine, I allowed the sickening reality of what had happened to sink in.

It was the beds, of course. A maid had talked to someone who talked to someone else and the porter was in on the gossip. Ruth was now steaming mad. Shoving aside my vestigial unease, I joined her: I no longer believed—though, God help me, I once had—that lesbians deserve to be spat upon at breakfast. It was a fine thing to be angry.

We settled our bill and went upstairs where we found the beds made up and returned to chaste separation. Grabbing our cases, we left the room and slammed the door shut behind us. As we crossed the dark, tiled hallway with its sofas and aspidistras, we noticed a pile of blankets lying on a table with a needle and thread beside them: a maid must have been darning them, working her way through the pile in the light of the floor lamp that glowed weakly in the corner. We stopped and looked at each other. Neither of us said a word as I leaned down and took the top blanket, folded it into a square and slipped it between our coats. We stalked out of the hotel, revved up the car and, still without saying a word, bumped over the cobblestones and headed north.

And that should have been the end of it—except that all the way to the border, breathtaking coves on our right and olive groves to our left, I shook alternately with anger and alarm. With my eyes glued to the rearview mirror, I watched for pursuers. Approaching the frontier post, I expected to be seized and dragged from the car. No one calls out the police for an old, much-darned blanket, Ruth reassured me. And, of course, I knew it was true.

As we sped away towards Carcassonne, I turned on a local French music station and relaxed. I was not irrational enough to believe that Interpol would get involved. All the way back to England, we slept in our tent under the warm blanket with its neat repairs. And very matrimonial it was too.

WILD PATIENCE

IN THE seventies and early eighties, poetry was at the heart of the women's movement, haunted by Muriel Rukeyser's famous lines: "What would happen if one woman told the truth about her life? / The world would split open." We looked to our poets for inspiration, vision, and the courage to persist. Women who had never read a poem that wasn't a school assignment devoured the work of poets like Judy Grahn, Audre Lorde, Susan Griffin, and Adrienne Rich.

Among those who spoke most profoundly to me was Rich. Each time a new book of her poems appeared, I brought it home to savor the words slowly, with an excitement that prickled up the back of my neck. Although I admired her earlier work, it was *The Dream of a Common Language* that struck a deep chord, especially "Transcendental Etude." "No one ever told us we had to study our lives / make of our lives a study, as if learning natural history / or music . . ." She knew the necessity and the terror of cutting ourselves adrift from our old lives before we had created new ones: ". . . We cut the wires, / find ourselves in free-fall, as if / our true home were the undimensional / solitudes, the rift / in the Great Nebula."

I'd already been shaken up by *Women and Honor: Some Notes on Lying*, an essay Adrienne had published as a chapbook, which plumbs the possibilities of honesty between women. We had all lied in the many ways women are forced to lie to survive. I had also spent years lying about my lesbianism, with words and with silence. With friends and lovers, I had been both liar and lied to; I knew, from both sides, about the harm caused by avoiding or burying hard truths, the loneliness it created. Yet I had felt an almost irresistible urge towards honesty, even when it felt too dangerous. "The unconscious wants truth" was like a neon sign to me. As I pondered *Some Notes on Lying*, I could almost feel the molecules in my body shifting uncomfortably, trying to rearrange themselves. Sentences like this one knocked me sideways: "An honorable human relationship—that is, one in which two people have the right to use the word 'love'—is a process, delicate, violent, often terrifying . . . a process of refining the truths they can tell each other." And this: "When a woman tells the truth she is creating the possibility for more truth around her." My first book of poems would come out in the mid-eighties; I titled it *Trying to Be an Honest Woman*.

These books exploded into our lives. They sent shock waves rippling across the country by way of feminist newspapers and journals, women's bookstores, and women's studies departments, copies becoming dog-eared as they passed from hand to hand. We quoted them in conversations, shared them in letters to friends, and read them aloud to each other. Lovers were wooed with the "Twenty-One Love Poems," which also provided the words for numerous important occasions. Once, Ruth and I had two lines piped on an anniversary cake for friends—a couple who had made it through what seemed at the time an astonishing five years: "Two women together is a work / nothing in civilization has made simple." Much hilarity was provided by the bakery, which wrote underneath the quote: "Adrienne and Rich." Ruth quickly swiped out the "and" and licked it off her finger.

AT THE end of 1981, I was teaching a course on women writers at PSU when I got a call from a woman at Reed College, inviting me to teach a class on Rich the following January. Adrienne would be giving a reading there in February from *A Wild Patience Has Taken Me This Far*, her most recent book; Ruth and I already knew the poems intimately.

I doubt that either one of us, on our own, would have had the nerve to act on what might have seemed to others a crazy idea. We didn't know Adrienne. I had only once, very briefly, been introduced to her at a conference. But in our universe of two, we didn't hesitate. I wrote inviting her to stay with us instead of being put up at the college or at a hotel when she came to Portland for her reading. I must have said that my apartment was simple and a little on the funky side, but it was quiet, the bed was comfortable, and she would have it to herself, while we would stay a block away at Ruth's. I assured her we would take good care of her. We knew that already, at fifty-two, she had limited mobility and was in constant pain from rheumatoid arthritis.

Adrienne replied immediately. "What a wonderfully hospitable letter. I'd been dreading the Reed part of that trip because it comes at the end and I'm hoping my energy will last. The offer of an apartment and informal company is very appealing."

Her next letter, replying to my questions about food and her schedule, opened with, "It feels wonderful to know I'll be in some kind of real situation in Portland, not just in the never-land of the travelling poet." She explained that she could not easily climb stairs or manage low chairs and beds, then went on to say that she knew she would feel at home with us, if only "because your face has been looking at me all year from our SW office wall." I can't quite imagine now, from a distance of four decades, why my face would have been on her *Sinister Wisdom* wall, unless it was on a poster advertising an issue that included my poems.

As it happened, her face had been looking at me all year from a wall beside my desk. In the matted but unframed photograph I'd inherited from Melanie Kaye-Kantrowitz when I took over her apartment,

Adrienne is perhaps in her early forties, looking both forceful and gentle. She's half-smiling, but it is her eyes that are compelling: they go straight to the heart of whatever she's looking at, missing nothing. At the same time, there's a kindness there.

We never doubted that we would feel at home with her too. If there was any nervousness—and there was some—it was because we were more than a little in awe of her; and we had not just invited her over for tea, we had invited her to *stay with us*—indeed, to spend *two days* with us. I had been writing poetry and publishing in feminist journals for a while, but perhaps even more than by poetry, we were connected by feminism. Adrienne understood that we had reached out to her in friendship, though in that era we would have called it sisterhood.

The night before she arrived, Ruth and I stayed up late trying to make my modest apartment fit for our guest. We washed a heap of mismatched dishes in the sink and then considered the bathroom with its pink tub, toilet and sink, and pink and purple plastic tiles. There wasn't a lot we could do with it, but at least we thought the tile would look better clean, so we spent several hours scrubbing it with tooth-brushes—something we wouldn't have dreamed of doing under any other circumstances. As I wielded my toothbrush up and down a chan-nel of grout, encrusted with years of soap and human residue, I started to see white spots dancing in front of my eyes, a sure sign of a migraine waiting to plow into my skull. Please, not now! I muttered, why do they always come at the worst time? We tidied up, made the bed, and put a vase of flowers on the desk.

All spruced up, my apartment had its good points: a roomy living area with a large bay window that looked out onto grass, just begin-ning its spring growth. There were trees, too, including a peach tree, holding on tightly to curled new leaves. Adrienne would be smack in the middle of "the lesbian zip code," a once middle-class part of town, now a little shabby, with turn-of-the-century "Old Portland" houses and their wisteria-covered porches, mixed in with newer apartment buildings. A friend lived in the house next door and often waved to me as I wrote at my desk in the bay. Adrienne might catch sight of her through the windows, running around starkers, as she was quite apt to do. Ruth's place was nicer, but we would use it for meals and hanging out; no one ever cooked in my kitchen.

WHILE RUTH was preparing a feast for dinner I made my way to the airport, parked in the parking garage, and found the gate where Adrienne's plane was due. I was thirty minutes early, buzzing with nervous energy and throbbing with migraine. I watched the plane land and eyed the passengers streaming up the jetway, the line gradually thinning out until a few stragglers, dragging carry-ons and sleepy children behind them, stumbled out and headed home.

I sat down in the empty waiting area, trying to think what to do. I was just considering finding a pay phone when a wheelchair appeared, pushed by an airport assistant. And there was Adrienne—very small, huddled in the chair with a thick wool coat and a briefcase piled on top of her. I leaped up as she broke into a smile, extricated a hand from her stuff and waved vigorously, her dark, almost black, eyes glittering. I was momentarily stunned to see her in a wheelchair; that wasn't how I had imagined her arrival. But it was only an airport chair, which she left at the curb, relying on a walking stick during her stay with us.

That evening swirls in my memory, many details drowned out by the pain in my head. I know that Adrienne happily unpacked in my bedroom and that I helped her up the steps at Ruth's, where the Norway maple was still spreading bare branches over the front lawn. She and Ruth immediately fell into animated conversation.

I probably avoided most of the dinner, protecting my stomach from the migraine, but I'm certain I didn't avoid the precious hours in front of the fireplace, the flames throwing a warm light onto our faces as we talked about books and movement politics. Although at first I remained quiet, thankful for Ruth's easy sociability, at some point I perked up as we began to talk more personally.

We were well into our second bottle of wine when Adrienne started to tell us about her partner, Michelle, who was working on a new novel, then moved on to describe their life in western Massachusetts. The freezing winters in Montague, she said, were contributing to the wretchedness of her disease; the two of them were considering moving to a more benign climate. Later, Adrienne asked if I was planning to stay in the US and Ruth told her we were in a quandary—we didn't know yet which of our two countries we would make our home in.

This led us to London and to Adrienne and Michelle's recent trip, where they had searched for Mary Wollstonecraft's grave, circling round and around St Pancras graveyard until they were exhausted, without managing to find it. We'll be there in the fall, I told her. We'll look for it. And when we find it, I grinned at her, we'll send you a photo.

I've forgotten the rest of what we talked about but the feel of it has stayed with me—how the conversation surged eagerly or drifted quietly, erupting with an occasional raucous moment. Ruth's dog, Rachel, and my Sheba slept at our feet, their ears twitching at bursts of laughter. Adrienne would echo my sense of it in a letter to us, a few weeks later: "I still feel warmed and exhilarated by the flow of talk we were all able to have during my stay in Portland—how I hope we can do it again before too long!"

It was getting late and I kept thinking Adrienne would want to go to bed, but she refilled her wine glass and brought up one new topic after another. Finally, I asked what she would like to do the next day.

"Is there any possibility," she said, "of a hot tub? It does wonders for the pain."

"No problem," I told her. And it wasn't.

BY THE morning, my head was clear, my vision sharp. After a late break-fast, I drove Adrienne in my little orange Datsun to Everett House, an unpretentious place in our neighborhood "dedicated to tranquility, in-ner peace, and overall community well-being." She leaned heavily on my arm as we climbed a few steps to the entrance and checked in with a patchouli-scented young woman.

Outside, there was a bench, still damp from a dawn shower, and a line of pegs under a small roof for our clothes. Adrienne looked at the bench and decided to remain on her feet. She took off her jacket and hung it up, calling me back from where I was wandering: "Judith, I'm going to need you to help me." Now that my migraine had fled, I was feeling strong and competent, but when it became clear that I would have to undress her, I was momentarily at a loss. One of the bless-ings of a lesbian community for me was becoming comfortable with women discarding their clothes. I had shed my inherited propriety and now enjoyed the naked cheerfulness of swimming pool locker rooms and communal showers—but this was Adrienne Rich.

She unzipped her pants, and I bent over to take off her shoes and socks while she leaned on my back. Gingerly, I helped her off with everything else and escorted her to the edge of the sunken tub. We stood there in cold spring sunlight, steam rolling up in front of us and swirling around our heads until we were in our own little cloud. I tested the railing and wondered out loud how she could get in safely. Together, we blew out hot breath and agreed that I'd better take off my own clothes, get into the water, and hold on to her, while she inched down the steps.

As soon as I was ready, Adrienne grasped the railing and took the first steps down. When she let go, I reached out both hands and slipped them under her arms. Holding her firmly, I felt her ribs press-ing into my forearms. A moment later, she tipped forward and her whole weight, small and frail as it was, pressed into me, skin to skin. I felt a sudden rush of compassion. Hardly wanting to release her, I set her down gently and felt my legs grow hot, as if they were blushing for my whole self. We settled on the wide ledge, swirling currents massaging us gently. Adrienne moved against a jet and rested her head on the rim of the tub with her eyes closed. She looked so peaceful that I copied her, and soon was listening to birds singing to one another high on the wall of bamboo.

In the afternoon the three of us picked up the threads of the previous night's conversation, pausing only for Adrienne to take a quick nap. I seized a few moments of quiet to write in my journal, wanting to record her willingness to need us as well as to be important to us.

I don't know if it was then, or during the night, that she bled onto my sheets, but I remember her confessing it to me, with an embarrassment she had not exhibited during our hot tub escapade. She mumbled something about heavy periods. Afterwards, I wondered if she was approaching menopause.

CROWDS BEGAN to converge on the long, red brick buildings of Reed. They hurried across the sweeping lawns, where students and their dogs went on playing frisbee and, although it was too chilly to picnic at the tables in the middle of the quad, people waiting for the reading sat there anyway, talking excitedly. Some were obviously students, a few of whom I recognized from the class I had taught. From the community, lesbians of every stripe far outnumbered everyone else. Ruth and I nodded, greeted, and waved to friends and acquaintances, while making our way through the crowd to grab our seats before we went to find Adrienne, whom we had dropped off earlier for a gathering with students and faculty.

We'd promised that we would wait backstage with her, and as soon as she saw us approaching, she beckoned. "Quickly," she said, leading the way into a women's bathroom where she produced a silver flask from her coat pocket, unscrewed the lid, took a long swig of rye, and handed it on. We huddled there, hastily passing the flask around, reveling in a moment's naughtiness while keeping our eyes on the door.

Adrienne read from *A Wild Patience* to a packed hall. I can still hear the collective sighs at the end of each poem and see Adrienne's powerful presence, growing larger as she stood, so still, in front of us. Towards the end, she read "Integrity," perhaps my favorite poem in that book. At the last line, "the skin these hands will also salve," she allowed the normally low pitch of her voice to drop even lower and acquire a hint of tenderness. The collective exhale became a hum, as if we were all savoring something delicious.

It wasn't hard to pry her loose from her last, lingering admirers; she was more than ready for dinner, and we had a table waiting for the three of us at Jake's, a long-established downtown restaurant with dark wood paneling and old-style waiters wearing long, white aprons. We were well into dessert, still high from the reading, when our friend Marian, a chiropractor, spotted us in our discreet booth and came over to chat. We'd been encouraging Adrienne to add alternative healthcare to the allopathic care she relied on, and to make changes to her diet; a few of her friends, including Tillie Olsen, had been doing the same. Marian was full of advice and stressed the importance of moving to a friendlier climate. (Three weeks later, Adrienne wrote to say that she and Michelle had decided to move to Santa Cruz on a trial basis, to see if they could live there. She had set up a massage therapist, an Alexander technician, an acupuncturist, and a nutritionist.)

When we got back to my place, it was well past one o'clock and we were all more than a little drunk. Adrienne took an arm from each of us and, moving in step like three Rockettes, we negotiated the porch stairs and danced her into the living room. I started to say good night but Adrienne reached up, pulled our heads towards her and breathed amiably, "I love you both." Soon we would receive a thank-you note, no doubt written in the more sober light of day, "I returned home in better shape than I left, and your hospitality (space, talk, food, drink, hot tubs) had much to do with it." Still, we never forgot the boozy "I love you."

ALL THROUGH the next decade we kept in touch. She sent us postcards hastily describing the move to Santa Cruz, improvements to her health, and upcoming surgeries. When Ruth started The Eighth Mountain Press, Adrienne was excited and wrote a long introduction to one of the press's first poetry books.

She sent tickets to a reading and reception in Seattle, writing that she was booked solid but "I do hope to get at least a look at you both." There were two thousand people in the University of Washington ballroom, all riveted by the poet. As usual there were no jokes. No chat. Nothing to woo the audience into liking her—no words to soften her fierceness. After all, this was the woman who had written: "The longer I live the more I mistrust / theatricality, the false glamour cast / by performance."

I sent her *Trying to Be an Honest Woman*, which she acknowledged with an affectionate note, focusing on the sequence, "Four Days in Spain." Those poems tell of my sister and me driving from Barcelona to Gibraltar to arrange for a headstone in the cemetery where our parents had recently been buried. We played in the ocean, and in the car, sang the songs we both knew, but we never talked about them.

Later I sent her a tape of a reading I'd given which happened to fall on her birthday. It included a sequence I was working on, "Villanelles for a Drowned Parent," which would eventually be included in my second book, *History and Geography*. She wrote to thank me for thinking of her birthday and said she was happy to know I'd been reading that night. Then came the words that left me rooted to the spot, holding my breath. "It was extremely moving to me to hear the villanelles," Adrienne wrote. "I think your work will always have to address that event at its deepest core, and when you work with it directly, your strongest & most poignant writing comes forth. Not that I imagine that is easy or can be happening all the time. But you have shown that you have the courage to keep going back—& it will not be simply the rehearsing of old trauma & loss, it will grow in you in new ways, & in your writing."

Like most teenagers who experience such a traumatic loss, I hadn't grieved at the time; I simply didn't have the emotional resilience. Instead, I indulged in excessive drinking, casual sex, and driving my sports car at hair-raising speeds on mountain roads, all in pursuit of defeating the numbness, trying to feel alive.

Now, in my mid-thirties, feeling foolish for having taken so long, I was beginning to wade into my grief. I had been trying, for years, to write about my parents' deaths, but first I needed to make my way through a thicket of fear, anger, profound sadness, and guilt at not being able to save them. So far, I'd managed only to write about avoiding grief.

"Villanelles for a Drowned Parent" was a step forward. The tightly structured poetic form allowed me, for the first time, to direct my pen straight into the "deepest core" of my loss and make poetry from it. Adrienne asked for a paper copy, which in due course she returned to me, copiously marked up in purple ink with a cover letter beginning, "I hope the enclosed doesn't look too forbidding to you. It's because I do care about what you're trying to do here that I took the time to think about what seems to me to hold the poems back, where that happens."

With Adrienne's prodding and grounded by my relationship with Ruth, I would go on to write a memoir, *Lifesaving*, and many more poems about becoming a teenage orphan. And Adrienne was right—it wasn't easy. It took me almost a decade to write *Lifesaving*, suffering more migraines than I'd ever had before. I had to keep stopping to recover before I plunged back in. The worst time was while I was writing the last part, in which I try to imagine my parents' last days on the burning ship, after most of the passengers and crew had left on lifeboats. They, along with about a hundred others, were left stranded onboard. As the fire raced across the decks, they had to climb down a ladder into the midnight sea. Getting so close to this scene, I grew nauseous, couldn't eat or sleep, and became impossible to live with—so I'm told.

Adrienne's note of encouragement ended with, "You could so easily have settled to be a charming, witty lesbian poet, period, with these caverns and reaches untouched for fear of too much pain & foreboding."

AS THE reputation of The Flight of the Mind spread, we were able to offer two week-long sessions, with workshops led by sought-after writers including Grace Paley, Lucille Clifton, Gish Jen, and Ursula Le Guin. We hoped to lure Adrienne to teach a class there. Of course, she was always busy, and I knew how difficult it was for her to travel. Still, in the fall of 1990, I was hopeful when I wrote to offer her a teaching week and a riverside cabin to herself the following summer. Not this time, she said—she already had too much on her plate and deadlines glaring at her; she urged us instead to hire Michelle, who was a Jamaican-American writer, known particularly in the feminist community for writing about being mixed-race. And so we did, gladly.

When the week began, everything seemed normal but slowly we slid into a *Twilight Zone* story; one thing after another revealed a darkness in Michelle—a bitterness and anger that was at odds with the optimistic, often joyful, atmosphere around her. Soon five of her students, young mixed-race women who had come specially to study with her, walked out of her class and refused to return.

Aware that some in her group were feeling humiliated and silenced by her, I had tried to talk with Michelle and each time found her at her cabin, in the morning before class, drinking directly from a bottle of booze, too inebriated to care. (Only later did we learn that her alcoholism was a not-very-well-kept secret.)

I wanted to fire her, but Ruth insisted it would make things worse. We left Michelle to the remains of her group, and I added a makeshift session for the distraught women and told them they could attend the next year without charge, travel expenses included.

Ruth and I stumbled through the days, exhausted from work and worry, determined that the debacle would not affect the other four classes. Without Ursula's sympathy and comforting—she witnessed it all with incredulity—we would have collapsed, weary and rattled. Flight had always been a relaxed, generous place, where women could take risks with their writing and feel safe getting to know those whose lives were unlike their own. In our cabin, the song of the river for once failing to soothe us, we spent sleepless nights trying to reconcile our respect and affection for Adrienne with these revelations about her partner. How could she be spending her life with someone like Michelle?

I had no energy left to worry about what it would mean for my friendship with Adrienne. But once home, I would soon find out. A furious and incoherent letter arrived from Michelle and then there were no more postcards or letters from Adrienne—no more invitations to send her my poems. As her silence grew longer, I gradually understood that she had chosen to stand with Michelle, and I understood why. Yet, some days when the mail thumped through the slot onto the floor I still looked to see if there was a postcard or an envelope addressed in her distinctive handwriting, containing a typed letter signed in ink with an elegant line under her name. When there was nothing, I turned away, feeling slightly sick. Our friendship had evaporated; the silence was absolute.

Nevertheless, Adrienne's work remained important to me. Every few years a new collection, or sometimes a selected or collected volume, would appear. I reviewed *Sources*, and continued to buy the books as soon as they came out. After *Your Native Land, Your Life*, I grew to expect each one to be a little more challenging than the last, as her subjects spread wider and the poetry became more complex. By 2004, with *The School Among the Ruins*, I had half a shelf of her poetry, much of it read and read again.

FIFTEEN YEARS had passed since I'd last heard from Adrienne, when, in 2006, I was contacted by Portland's Literary Arts, asking me to introduce her at an upcoming reading in their Downtown Poetry series. My first thought was to turn them down; they clearly had no idea that Adrienne might not welcome it. But the more I mulled it over, the more I wanted to contribute, in some small way, to the success of her reading, and also, to acknowledge our past relationship. It flashed through my mind that this might be the last time I saw her, and it was.

Over the years, I had found help and support from other poets, briefly from Amy Clampitt and then from Maxine Kumin, whose work I loved and whose friendship endured longer than Adrienne's—Max's last note to me about my poems coming within weeks of her death. But Adrienne's engagement with my poetry had come at a crucial time. I owed her a great deal and wanted to let her know both that I remained grateful, and that as a reader of her work, I had never retreated.

Close to the event, I was dismayed to learn that there would be a pre-reading dinner for Adrienne; important sponsors, board members, and a few local literary folk, including Ruth and me, were invited. I had hoped to offer up my olive branch at the reading, not over dinner, but we had to attend. At the Heathman Hotel, a long table across the end of the dining room was set for twelve; Adrienne and the director were seated in the middle on the far side when Ruth and I arrived and took our assigned places opposite them. As we pulled out our chairs, our old friend looked up, her penetrating eyes, that I had seen soften in her gentler moods, were more piercing than ever. A shadow passed over her face, she nodded at us then kept her gaze averted. Our good friend, the poet, Janice Gould, who was seated next to me, chatted eagerly with her and, little by little, with Janice's help, Ruth and I managed to enter the conversation. It was hard going and, by the time we all moved over to the church venue, I was heartily sorry I had agreed to do the introduction.

In the green room I greeted Adrienne cautiously. I had done nothing to deserve Michelle's fury, nor Adrienne's rejection, yet I was fighting an urge to hang my head. I kicked myself into action and asked her what she needed from me, which put us both on a practical footing. I could help her up the steps to the stage, she told me, and once onstage she would sit in the chair provided; this would be the first time she had ever given a seated reading, and she was worried that it wouldn't go over well. When she asked me to go outside and wait for her, I remembered the bathroom at Reed and smiled to myself. Time to pull out the flask?

Someone gave the microphone three taps and began to speak. I was being introduced as the poet who would, in turn, introduce Adrienne. I left her at the stage door then walked out to a round of applause, planted my feet in front of the mic, and took a deep breath. I spoke of Adrienne the poet and Adrienne the political activist. I asked why so many people today question whether "poetry matters" and, raising my voice, I said, "the work of Adrienne Rich, in any reasonable world, would put an end to that debate." I spoke personally about her kindness and what I had learned from her about being a writer, about craft, about the importance of holding to unshakable, humane values.

It was a long introduction. When I arrived at, "Please help me welcome one of our greatest poets, Adrienne Rich," she walked slowly across the stage to cheers and applause, planting her cane with each step, and stopping beside me. She reached up, gave me a brief hug, and looked me straight in the eye, with a hint of surprise and a smile. Holding up her hand to quiet the crowd she said, "Thank you for this incredibly warm welcome." Then, turning towards me, as I was leaving the stage, "And thank you, Judith, for your incredibly warm words."

UNBEKNOWNST TO her, Adrienne left me with one last gift. She became my model for keeping going when it's no longer easy.

In my fifties, I had finally been diagnosed with a genetic, neuromuscular, degenerative disease named after three doctors: Charcot Marie Tooth. There were early signs: sprained ankles and weakening muscles in my feet; a gradual loss of stamina. Undaunted, I learned to bandage my ankles so as to finish an important tennis match, and to borrow a friend's frozen peas to ice my painful feet when travelling.

The disease continued to progress—slowly, incrementally. By the time I was in my early sixties I could no longer keep up, without serious pain, walking with friends from a restaurant to a concert hall, and by my seventies I could only manage a block or two, so I traded my not-very-useful legs for the wheels of a mobility scooter. When the disease moved into my hands, writing became difficult and typing with certain fingers was a challenge; holding on tight to anything small, or just cold hands could set off painful cramps, rivaling the neuropathic pain that struck my feet at night. Long evenings even in good company had always exhausted me, but now they cut into my next day's work, setting up unenviable dilemmas. Over time, with help, I managed to learn how to ration my small gas tank of energy. I found a way to live, and live well, even with chronic pain.

At the time of Adrienne's visit, I was thirty-seven and still backpacking up Mount Adams, walking miles on trips abroad, playing tennis three times a week. I had little real understanding of the pain she endured and the energy she had to muster to live the life she chose. That comprehension kicked in the first time I needed a wheelchair in the airport, and grew in tandem with my increasing disability.

As my body began to succumb to Charcot Marie Tooth, I continued to travel to writing residencies and teaching gigs. It was sometimes rough. In Anchorage, where I taught in an MFA program, I once arrived on crutches, my injured leg wrapped from thigh to foot; in England, after a long journey to teach an Arvon workshop in Devon or in Yorkshire, I was worn out before the week began. Once, at the

Tyrone Guthrie Centre, after a grueling drive and a ferry ride across a stormy Irish Sea, my energy ran out before the end of my residency and I had to leave early. Even at Hedgebrook, on Whidbey Island, where I'd enjoyed good writing time before, I could no longer manage the loft ladder nor fit comfortably into the sleeping space below it.

Determined not to cave in to my limitations, I would think about Adrienne, arriving in Portland alone, in a wheelchair. I'd remember not only her indominable energy, good humor, and seriousness about what matters, but also her naked vulnerability in the hot tub, how she spoke openly about her disease, and how she asked for the help she needed. How, too, when she could no longer stand for a reading, she sat down. Most of all, I'd remember that she kept on writing, her work becoming more profound with every deeply mined volume.

VIRGINIA'S APPLE

LLYN, MY old housemate from Elgin Avenue, now sober, turned up unexpectedly in Portland for a short visit. One afternoon she mentioned that she had two friends in London who wanted to come to the Northwest for a longish visit and were looking to swap houses; when she left, I had a piece of paper on which she had jotted a woman's name and address.

Within a few days I had written to Sarah offering her the use of my apartment and my old orange Datsun. Ruth and I were somewhat surprised when she wrote back by return post saying that never once had she considered coming to Oregon—in fact she hardly knew where Oregon was. Nevertheless, she expressed enthusiasm for the idea.

So in the late summer of 1982, Ruth and I settled into the unaccustomed luxury of a terraced house in a rapidly gentrifying part of Islington. Outside, steps and pillars broadcast old elegance; inside it was faded in an English genteel kind of way: the armchairs were dusty and the fireplace in the sitting room had blackened the mantle above, where photographs, almost too small to decipher, stood in their motley frames. The basement kitchen was modern and bright and in the walled garden, soon to be littered with leaves and rotting tomatoes, there was a patio where it was still warm enough for us to eat breakfast with grapes dangling above our heads.

We'd clearly won the better deal, although my Datsun was marginally more comfortable than Sarah's wheezy blue Citroen 2CV, with its open-the-window air conditioning. Briefly we wondered how she would react to life in my dingy apartment, but soon forgot about her and her partner who were now, presumably, exploring my bookshelves while we browsed hers, pulling out volumes inscribed to Sarah's mother by authors of the Bloomsbury group. Photos and letters from Angelica, Bunny, and others fell into our laps as we opened the books.

We had five, or maybe it was six, weeks—a long time away from our everyday lives. I needed to be there, to hear the doves, read *The Guardian* every morning, and feel my body relax into human interactions that felt familiar. In Portland, my life had been overrun with meetings: meetings to plan protests against the Rose Festival, to mediate between lesbians and gay men, to study women's history, to examine my own prejudices. Sometimes I would rush from one to another in the same evening; I was relishing the thought of all the meetingless days ahead when I would be able to take long baths, topping up the hot water and reading until my fingers shriveled.

As usual, Ruth had been overworking as she shouldered the responsibility for another precedent-setting lawsuit, this one against a county sheriff for failing to arrest a violent husband. She'd won in the Oregon Supreme Court and after much kerfuffle, national publicity, and testifying before Congress, she would be only too happy to sleep late, catch up on pleasure reading, and wander around London and the narrow lanes of Sussex.

In the afternoons we meandered through the local outdoor markets, sometimes meeting my old friends, but more often making our destination one of the few monuments connected to women: Emmeline Pankhurst next to Parliament; Edith Cavill at Trafalgar Square; Boudica, the warrior Queen of the Iceni, standing tall behind her pair of horses at Westminster Bridge.

Feminist historians were beginning to unearth ordinary as well as extraordinary women's lives and we were avid readers of their work. We began to design our walks to take us by houses where interesting women had lived and worked: writers, artists, labor organizers, birth control campaigners, and suffragettes. These were rarely marked. There was nothing in Bishopsgate to mark the location of the 1888 "Matchgirl's Strike" when fourteen hundred women and girls stopped the factory and won concessions. Nor was there a marker at 58 Doughty Street, Holborn, where Vera Britain and Winifred Holtby lived. There was an old plaque at the Bloomsbury house where Christina Rossetti lived and died, and one for Elizabeth Barrett Browning at 50 Wimpole Street. But there was no mention of Sylvia Pankhurst at 20 Cheyne Walk, or Mary Shelley at 24 Chester Square, nor the "mouse castle" at 2 Campden Hill Square where suffragettes went to recover from their hunger strike in prison, after which they were rearrested and sent back (under the provisions of the Cat and Mouse Act). The house in Primrose Hill where Sylvia Plath took her life had a blue plaque that read "William Butler Yeats, 1865–1939, Irish poet and dramatist lived here." (It would be another three and a half decades before English Heritage launched its "Plaques for Women" campaign; 3 Chalcot Square now has a second blue plaque: "Sylvia Plath, 1932–1963, Poet, lived here 1960–1961.")

Since remaining friends with former lovers was more or less the law in lesbian circles, we saw Lilian, who was engaged in starting a lesbian-feminist press. One morning, we met her for a walk on Hampstead Heath; mercifully, she seemed, at least for now, to like Ruth rather more than me, which I assumed meant she'd be less likely to make trouble. I wanted to show Ruth the women's pond, scene of so many drowsy summer afternoons where a few rowdy—or randy—women used to pose on the raft out among the ducks while dozens of dykes sunbathed, quietly reading books by women. The sign still read: "Women and girl swimmers only. No men beyond this point."

Women were lying face down with their bikini tops unhooked and the sturdy lifeguard prowled around, just as she used to, watching out for a stray nipple. The grass held the imprints of generations and I knew my outline lingered on in the sunniest spot, probably still lush with the cooking oil I used to spread over my limbs.

We climbed the hill and sprawled among galloping dogs and ice-cream-licking kids. Lilian aimed her attention intensely at Ruth while I leaned back in the sun and plucked a long blade of grass to chew. After a while, we wandered off to Highgate Cemetery to see if we could find George Eliot's grave. Ruth had been rereading *Middlemarch*, and the preface had given a few hints about the location of her stone. It turned out to be in a section that wasn't open to the public and, after failing to find a groundskeeper to unlock the gate, we spotted an opening and squeezed in. We pushed through unruly shrubs and thigh-high grasses where wild foxes still lived until we made it to the path. Sure enough, right next to Eliot's stone was the marker Ruth had read about—the grave of her devoted friend, the sculptor Elma Stuart, who had insisted on being buried next to her.

One morning, the two of us set off to find Mary Wollstonecraft's grave in the churchyard of St Pancras Old Church. Unbeknownst to us, there are two St Pancras churches—one dating back to 1822 and the other to about 312 AD. We inspected the inscriptions of nearly all the stones in the wrong churchyard before finding the right one. Her monument is a great square chunk of stone. As we sat on the earth among purple blooms, its warm, slightly rough surface pressing into our backs, Ruth remembered Wollstonecraft's "melancholy emotions of sorrowful indignation." We felt a kind of euphoria sitting there, the sun pulling from the ground sweet aromas of earth and plant life that were a relief after the odors of human debris and dirty oil that hung around the nearby railway stations. Lingering, reluctant to leave, we took pictures of each other to document our presence. Nearly two hundred years had passed since *The Vindication of the Rights of Women* had been published; if only its author could know how she had inspired the courage and hard work of thousands of her readers. We were a part of that great effort and had come to believe that changing the world for women would be our life's work.

I WANTED to see the Gateways club in Chelsea, mentioned in numerous books about old-time dykes, and featured in *The Killing of Sister George*, the first film I'd ever seen that openly depicted lesbians. The scene where sexy Coral Browne seduces the lovely Susannah York away from her jolly district-nurse lover, Beryl Reid, jumped erratically where the censor had chopped out the good parts. Later I watched it twice more with that scene intact.

We considered inviting some of my old friends but decided against it. They wouldn't have shared my romantic view of it. The club had been picketed in the seventies by the Gay Liberation Front whose members stood outside in Bramerton Street chanting, "Out of the closet, into the streets," and then invaded the premises to pull the plug on the jukebox, leaving the regular patrons mystified.

Hauling black calf-length boots in my suitcase had hardly seemed worthwhile, but I pulled them on over my best jeans, and ran an iron over the burgundy tie I'd slipped in at the last minute. Having put on a school tie every day for years, I quickly made the knot and pushed it smoothly up into the hollow of my throat between the points of my black collar. Ruth had pulled a shot silk, purple top over her head and was crouching in front of the mirror to slip in dangling earrings and brush on a touch of mascara. As we walked out of the front door, she took my arm and we walked jauntily in step to the car. Then we drove off with the ghosts of Violet Trefusis and Radclyffe Hall hovering nearby.

The unobtrusive door on the side street off the King's Road was opened a crack by a bouncer who took a good look before opening wider and vetting us. I was looking down the narrow, steep stairs, at the bottom of which another door muffled the sound of music from within, when the beefy woman gave me a friendly slap on the back that almost precipitated me headfirst down to the bar.

As my eyes got used to the thick smoke, I could see women swaying together or eyeing each other on bar stools. I'd seen old photos of the 1930s clientele and retained images of women in creased pants and white shirts with slicked back DAs, and others in dresses with flared skirts and padded shoulders, their hair rolled back in a sausage from their foreheads. These 1980s dykes were much dowdier, although still recognizably attached to one role or the other. Most of them wore pants of some kind and, since it was hot, they had shed their jackets to display short-sleeved nylon-looking shirts, or a variety of frilly blouses. Down here in the dark, they seemed resigned, as if banished to an underground burrow; I imagined them emerging into the light and clamor of the street, blinking their eyes and ducking their heads, before scurrying off into anonymous lives. But who was that bouffant blonde in the darkest corner? Could it be Dusty Springfield? She was reputed to be a regular.

Ruth seemed a bit bemused at finding herself there, even though she was interested. She'd been taken to a gay bar in New York in the early seventies, back when you had to wear three articles of "women's clothing" and leave your ID at home in case of a police raid. For me, although it was undeniably depressing, it was also exhilarating. I didn't want to belong there, but in some mysterious way I felt that I did.

We ordered drinks from the bartender, a fiftyish woman who looked at us with curiosity. Then we stood up, clinging to one other more than actually making any moves that might be called dancing. I liked the feel of Ruth's silk shirt under my hand at the small of her back as I leaned over to rest my cheek against hers.

"Just imagine," I ventured into her ear. "This could have been my life if I'd been born even a few years earlier."

"Or if you hadn't managed to become one of those troublemakers," she said drily.

Aware that we were being watched, we pressed our bodies together, thighs and breasts sticky with heat. I looked around at these women who had failed to find the movements of our time, their secrets throbbing along with the lugubrious music. When the smoke became too much for us, we paid our tab and as we left the bouncer gave me a conspiratorial wink.

I LAY back with my head on Ruth's thigh at the top of the Devil's Dyke—the gorge outside Brighton that slices deeply through close-cropped hills dotted with sheep. This was country I'd explored on my horse when I was a teenager and knew intimately. The smell of grass mixed with a briny breeze blowing from the ocean, the gorse bushes still ablaze, and the distant shouts of tourists spilling from the bus at the Dyke Hotel, all were unchanged. For a moment I might have been that teenager again, lying with the sun on my face and Magic cropping the grass beside me.

We'd polished off the French bread, tomatoes, hunks of Cotswold cheese, and olives, and were sprawled sleepily across the tartan rug that served both for eating and napping on afterwards. When I woke up, Ruth was lying on her back emitting gentle snores. She'd placed her wire-rimmed glasses beside her on the rug, and her black hair rumpled in waves across her forehead, the silver threads catching the sunlight. Who would have thought that I'd be here now, my head resting on the blue jeans of a woman I acknowledged openly as my lover, as she did me? When she stirred and opened her eyes, I resisted the urge to look around before I leaned over and kissed her.

In the village of Rodmell, we walked down the narrow street past cottages with scarlet runner beans and roses. Lanes like this one, with the hump of the Downs rising like a sleeping beast in the distance, still featured in my dreams. Monk's House appeared on our right, the church spire hovering over its shoulder. Standing closer to the road than I'd expected, it seemed much too small. It wasn't yet open to the public, but Ruth calmly pushed open the wooden gate and walked in.

"There's no one here," she called.

I paced up and down outside the fence, catching glimpses of the garden while she peeped through the windows.

"Come and look—there's a vase here on the windowsill with the initials, VW. It's one of Vanessa's."

As she disappeared round the corner of the house, I kept watch, embarrassed and irritated.

"I can see Virginia's writing shed back here," she called in a loud voice.

I longed to see the garden where the two famous elms might still be standing; at the foot of one would be the inscription: "Beneath this tree are buried the ashes of Virginia Woolf: Born January 25, 1882; Died March 28, 1941. Death is the enemy. Against you I will fling myself unvanquished and unyielding—O Death. The waves broke on the shore." I took one step towards the gate but couldn't bring myself to go in.

Ruth returned, holding out an apple on the palm of her hand as if offering it to a horse.

"Oh Lord! Did you pick that off a tree?" I grumbled.

"Yes, sweetie, it's for you. One of Virginia's!"

It looked like a Cox's. That particular crispness would split open and spurt its sweet juice onto my taste buds.

"I can't," I said testily and, although aware of her bewilderment, went on, "How could you? In this country we don't just walk uninvited into people's gardens."

"Oh, for heaven's sake" she said, "don't be ridiculous."

When you fall in love, you are stunned to discover that the two of you are uncannily alike, that you share an unusual number of interests and opinions, and that everything you do with the other is brighter, clearer, more profound. But then comes the creeping awareness of how different you are. Loving the soulmate is a lot easier than learning to love the stranger.

Neither of us wanted to have an argument at Monk's House, so we wandered down the lane without speaking, gradually starting to breathe more easily. It was an afternoon of clover and weak English sun. As we retraced our steps past the church, we managed to shake off the sense of finding each other incomprehensible. All it took was a rueful smile and the touch of a hand on a hand. It would be a long time before we came to understand that our different sensibilities could be a gift that gave each of us another set of eyes with which to look at the world.

Stepping carefully around the fresh cowpats left by the herd that had recently trudged down to the milking barn, we were stopped by an old man in muddy gardening trousers and Wellington boots.

"Looking for the Woolf house, are you?" he said. "Knew it well in their day, I did!" Clearly, he was dying to tell us about it.

"Mrs. Woolf," he said, "she was a lovely lady. I remember her coming out of the gate in her long skirt after the cows went down in the afternoon." He paused for effect.

"Mrs. Woolf would hold up her skirt like this," (he pinched his thumb and forefinger together) "and make her way between the piles of . . . *evidence*. She would nod her head and say to me: "'Good afternoon, Mr. Winters. Very *rural* around here today, isn't it?'"

I imagined the tall woman, so familiar from photographs, setting up her outdoor table with cups and saucers and the silver teapot with its slightly bent finial. There would be a phut-phut-phut as Vita's motorcar puttered down the lane. And here she came, striding into the garden in her buttoned breeches, a tweed jacket falling open across her cream blouse—Vita so clearly the lesbian. Virginia the . . . what? Well, at least for this afternoon, Virginia, too, fitted that description, as she passed a custard cream biscuit to her lover and took off into one of the famous flights of eloquence that served her so well as flirtation.

The River Ouse with its relentless current flowed nearby, hidden by trees. Beyond it and up the hill, my family, long ago, used to take Sunday walks on the springy turf, and just downstream from here my school once brought us on a field trip to observe the lower reaches meandering towards the sea. I had stretched out on the grass that day, shedding my blazer and Panama hat, and drawn diagrams of oxbow lakes in my geography notebook, never realizing how close I was to the author whose words would come to mean so much to me—whose honesty in her diaries and memoirs would inspire me to find words for my own secrets.

I loved pottering around Sussex with Ruth in the valiant *deux chevaux*, one day pointing out the cottage where Colin's mother had lived—and maybe still did, though I had no way of knowing—and another day stopping in Edburton to look at the smoked fish business Colin had long since left behind. It was a flourishing shop now, with a well-advertised smoker catering to the upscale bankers and solicitors who commuted to London from their faux farms. The sloping displays showed off oak-smoked salmon and kippers as well as the eels that Colin had once so painstakingly trapped. On one of the walls, above spotless white tiles, hung framed photographs depicting the history of Springs' Smoked Salmon: and there he was, smiling shyly in his white fishmonger coat and Wellington boots.

One day, we drove past Wiston Pond, where my father used to fish for trout. In my tree-climbing ninth year, I tumbled out of a willow right into the water, but my father's frustration had more to do with my scaring off the fish than with my bruised, weed-draped body emerging from the shallows. On these drives we spun out stories from our lives—there was so much we didn't yet know about each other—and sometimes sang songs: old Beatles and Bob Dylan hits, melodramatic renditions of Dusty Springfield favorites, or the Hebrew rounds Ruth tried to teach me. She was keen to acquire Britishisms like "I've got your number, duckie!" which she flung out zanily. I was fond of the BBC quiz shows on the radio, especially *Brain of Britain*, throughout which I would demand no talking and fiddle with the tuning knob. Ruth was intrigued by *Yesterday in Parliament* with its raucous argument and clever repartee. Mostly, though, we talked and talked. Once a friend told us that when she and her husband traveled, they ran out of things to say and would sit at dinner dredging up only the dullest small talk. Ruth and I never ran out of things we wanted to talk about, tell or ask each other, and forty-five years later we still prefer one another's company to any other.

THE IVY that covered so many houses was beginning to show red as we drove into Henfield. I had known the area well when Colin and Roddy lived down the road and I'd ridden Frank across neighboring fields or along the cart tracks that linked up the farms. Ruth and I entered the village, interested to look at Backsettown, a large house Elizabeth Robins, the author of the recently reissued novel, *Votes for Women*, had shared with Octavia Wilberforce, a descendent of the famous antislavery family. Octavia had been Virginia Woolf's physician and in wartime, with its food shortages and rationing, she had sent regular gifts of cream from her Jersey herd over to Monk's House. The two of them had left the property in trust as a rest home for working women to get out of London and recuperate from overwork or illness, and it had been functioning as such for the past thirty years.

Someone directed us up a lane between crumbling stone walls; someone else pointed us past the cricket pitch and towards the common. Finally, a farm hand gestured up another lane and we pulled into a gateway from which we caught sight of the house. I climbed over the five-bar gate to get a clearer view and a Jersey cow shoved its leathery nose into my hand. The rest of the herd grazed peacefully, long eyelashes drooping over moist marble eyes. Their hair was chestnut and the hollows in their flanks warm. You could have nestled your cheek there in front of the hipbone, but probably no one ever had—except perhaps Octavia when she had hand-milked their ancestors. But when we crossed the field, a matron strode out to see us off the premises: there was *absolutely no visiting*.

We made our way to Henfield's modest museum to see what they might have on Octavia and Elizabeth, and a white-haired man directed us across the street to the curator Lucy Bishop's house, where we climbed the steps and tapped with the brass knocker. The small, hunchbacked woman of perhaps ninety who opened the door, smiled sideways up at us.

"Come in, come in," she said when we started to tell her what we were looking for. Then, as we stood in the doorway, she turned towards the garden and called in a surprisingly robust voice, "Diana, we have visitors!"

A slightly younger woman stuck her head in through a window and called out, "How'd you do. You must stay for tea. I'll come in and make a pot."

In the sitting room with its dark sideboard and well-worn armchairs, we had given an enthusiastic account of our interest in Elizabeth and Octavia and were making good inroads into the sponge cake too, when there was another knock at the door. It was flung open before either of our hosts could move from her chair, and two women marched in, the leader, also an octogenarian, tweed skirted and leather brogued, brandishing a book.

"Look what I got," she said with some triumph. "It's just out from The Women's Press: the latest in feminist theory by Dale Spender." Then she noticed us.

"These two," said Lucy, "found us in their pursuit of Wilberforce and Robins."

"How splendid," said Patience Ropes, who, we would later learn, had been a highly regarded literary agent.

As we listened to a string of tales, including one we didn't entirely follow about a young woman who had once raised goats on the common and walked many miles to early Women's Institute meetings, we glanced meaningfully at each other. We had stumbled into the middle of Henfield's lesbian community—one that went back a hundred years or more—whose existence I had never dreamed of. I can't quite grasp, even now, what it would have been like if, at fourteen or fifteen, I'd come across them greeting the neighbors as they shopped at the butcher's and the greengrocer's. Ruth raised an eyebrow at me very slightly: we'd have to talk about it all later.

"Have you heard about the Lavender Ladies?" Lucy asked. "They lived in that cottage just behind the common—you can't miss it, it's thatched and there's lavender lining the path from the picket gate to the front door. They had a flourishing business making soaps and eventually became suppliers to the royal family."

Lucy looked as if she had, all by herself, snared the Buckingham Palace account. "You know—'By Appointment to His Majesty.'"

"It's *Her* Majesty now, dear," said Diana gently.

"I know, I know." Lucy sounded a little irritated. "I was talking about King Edward VII."

"Well, the point is," Patience interjected, "they only ever employed other women." She paused. "No men at all." Another long pause as looks were exchanged all around the room. Finally, Diana picked up the teapot and bustled to the kitchen to make a fresh pot.

After tea, Patience insisted that we follow her and Helen to their house to see some paintings by Gluck, a woman whose name we didn't recognize.

"I often used to run into her on the train up to town," Patience told us as we walked along the High Street and turned a corner to her bungalow. "She was obsessed with getting the government to set standards for oil paints. Masterpieces would be lost to the future, she used to say. She spent far too much time on that. Should have been painting more of her own masterpieces."

While Helen poured us drinks, Patience showed us two of Gluck's paintings and insisted on giving us catalogues for past shows. The oval table on which we placed our glasses had once belonged to Radclyffe Hall, she told us matter-of-factly. Of course, the author would have owned tables, beds, silver cream jugs, and monogrammed handkerchiefs; I knew that. But this very table? It was well polished, cherry perhaps, or some wood that glowed with a reddish patina, and as taste-ful as befitted a lesbian who had her suits made by a Jermyn Street tailor. And then, as would happen a few times during these weeks, the very substance of an object—the curve of its legs, the solidity of its flat surface—gave its one-time owner a new kind of substance too.

Years later, when we had lunch with the poets Ursula Fanthorpe and Rosie Bailey at their Gloucestershire home, Rosie mentioned that the table we were sitting at had belonged to Radclyffe Hall: Ursula and Rosie had inherited it from Patience. Running my hand across the polished surface, I had a sense that Ruth must be feeling some-thing similar to what I felt at that moment as I saw us both being car-ried along in the slipstream of all those independent women, rabble-rousers, cross-dressers—generation after generation of lesbians.

WE HAD crossed England from Beatrix Potter's Lake District to Barbara Hepworth's St Ives (where Talland House was now holiday flats). We'd followed Gluck's footsteps along the Coast Path to the artists' colony at Lamorna Cove and hunched over, peering at gravestones on the floor of Winchester Cathedral, only to find that someone had forgotten to mention that Jane Austen was a writer. We'd tracked down Sylvia Plath at Court Green in Devon and searched unsuccessfully for Vanessa Bell's Charleston, not yet open to the public. We were so bitten by this bug of finding women's history in the landscape that we pursued *Orlando* through many of the three hundred and sixty-five rooms of Vita Sackville-West's Knole, the ancestral home she had been unable to inherit by virtue of her sex. When we went on to Sissinghurst, the "two *mädchens*" who featured in Vita's diary were still tending the famous garden.

We were reluctant to let go of this intoxicating search for what Adrienne Rich had called "the spirit of place," but it would come back to grip us time and time again. One year, on a trip through France, heading for Spain, as we sat in a village square drinking our early-morning coffee, we noticed an old postcard stand, holding faded pictures of George Sand, whose country home, Villa Algira, stood on the River Creuse at nearby Gargilesse. Naturally, we made a detour to see the house. To our delight, years later we found the writer again in Mallorca, at the monastery in Valldemossa where she'd spent a miserably cold winter with her lover, Chopin.

Another year I was invited to teach a writing workshop on the Greek island of Lesbos. Afterwards we drove in a rented car across the island through a wild, rocky landscape to Eresos, where Sappho is reputed to have been born. Walking along the stony beach, I picked up a smooth, pink pebble, telling myself that maybe Sappho's foot had, 2,700 years ago, stepped right there.

We had lunch next to the beach with crashing waves flinging spray at us and a windstorm tugging at the canopy overhead. The village was full of lesbians—the people of Lesbos as well as our kind who were mostly European and more stylish than the American variety. Mary Barnard, one of the great translators of Sappho, who lived near us in Oregon and whom I had known, had died a few days earlier. Quickly, I wrote one of her Sappho fragments on a scrap of paper and tacked it to the bulletin board outside the Sappho Hotel.

You may forget but

Let me tell you
this: someone in
some future time
will think of us.
      —SAPPHO

THE CHILL in the air hinted that our summer trip was over, and we decided to spend our last few days hiking the South Downs Way. The sun was gleaming on the Sussex countryside as we set off from Falmer, climbing steadily up the path beside wheat fields with their new military buzz cuts. The muscles in my calves began to protest as the hill grew steeper and we negotiated a couple of stiles, leaving the stubble behind and stepping onto the open hilltop where the path faded into smooth turf. The sun disappeared and the wind picked up as we passed one bent rowan tree pointing a crooked finger towards Kent. Just as we reached the ridgeline, everything grew dark, and we walked into a sheet of rain. We dumped our borrowed backpacks on the grass and rummaged, looking for the ponchos that, of course, were at the bottom. Socks, underwear, spare sweaters, all were soggy by the time we refastened the laces and pulled the ponchos over our heads. We walked on but finally stopped again; wind was blowing the rain up the side of the downs, inflating the ponchos like balloons and soaking our clothes underneath. In the space of an hour, we had walked out of a country calendar and into a bad dream.

Ruth shouted something that was hard to hear. I caught the words "pub" and "fireplace" and nodded enthusiastically.

We sloshed down the north face of the Downs, slipping on patches of bare chalk and wading through muddy gateways until we reached Underhill Lane. In Poynings, we did, indeed, find a pub with a fireplace beside which we steamed gently while we wolfed a ploughman's, scotch eggs, and lagers.

It was not much after two and we lingered there, putting off the unappealing return to the blustery top of the Downs. After a while I persuaded Ruth that the lane winding along the foot of the escarpment would be less exposed: Ditchling was only six miles away and had a couple of promising B&Bs in our Ramblers Handbook. But six miles is a long way when the rain is pouring off the front of your hood in a steady stream, your pack is digging into your shoulders, and your feet squelch with every step. The road was barely wide enough for two cars to pass, and each time one whizzed by at the speed all cars dash around those lanes, it threw water mixed with mud and cow dung over us.

When we heard one approaching from behind, we jumped into the ditch or scuttled into a gateway. Soon the world was reduced to the placing of one foot in front of the other, our eyes watching only the ground directly ahead. Rain drummed on ponchos and feet acquired a rhythm to which songs began forming in my mind. Once in a while, cows heaved themselves onto their hoofs and approached their fences, lowing seductively to be taken inside for milking or for a nice warm something. By the time we reached the B&B, set back from the lane behind a hedge, we were too tired and discouraged to go out again. We snuggled together under the duvet until morning, making do with a packet of biscuits.

The next evening, after more hours of trudging along, cold and wet, and a blissful fifteen minutes squashed between sacks of horse pellets inside a chatty farmer's van, we found a pub on the main street of Steyning that offered us a room up in the attic—a small triangle with sloping beams way too low for my six-foot frame, but there was an electric fire and we collapsed into bed, grateful to drag off our boots. During the night, I woke in the grip of severe menstrual cramps and staggered to my pack, banging my head on the way, to retrieve three potent pain pills. Ruth, a frequent insomniac, was awake. I groaned and pointed at my ovaries. She sighed sympathetically and held out her arms.

Ruth pulled out of her pack the one book we had brought with us, a slightly damp copy of short stories by Andrea Dworkin. She rolled against me and started to read aloud. Neither of us particularly liked the stories but the sound of Ruth's voice was soothing. Giving up on the book, we wrapped our legs around each other's and made it through the night, talking, crying, dozing, and then talking again, while the rain landed on the skylight in uneven bursts, beating hard for a while and then easing off to a soothing patter. In the darkness, the ghosts of all our longings hovered between us and around us.

By morning, Ruth had a terrible cold and I was well on my way into a migraine. White-faced and nauseous, I lay in the bathtub, oddly located in a corner of the room, while Ruth went downstairs to see what she could scare up to eat. The rain, now banging rudely on the roof, was relentless. Walking was clearly out of the question, but we refused to give up entirely. We would take three buses back to fetch the car and then continue on following the South Downs Way—though God knows why.

The steamy shelter of the old Citroen was a blessing and by the time we approached the village of Bury, the squeaky windshield wipers were sweeping away rain that had become only a light mist. We pushed open the gate to a thatched B&B posing in a picture-book rose garden. The carved front door swung open and a welcoming elderly couple offered herb teas and a large room with aromatic sachets on the pillows and hot-water bottles between embroidered sheets. The woman draped all our damp garments above the Aga in the kitchen to dry; then, clucking over Ruth's stuffed-up head, sent her off to recover under a goose-feather quilt, promising breakfast in bed the next morning.

Exhausted, I sank into a chaise longue in the conservatory, where tentative sunlight was beginning to warm the damp air, and fell fast asleep. When I opened my eyes, it was dusk and I could hear doves calling from the dovecot and our hostess pottering around in the kitchen. Although nothing in my life had exactly resembled this scene with its whiff of fairy tale, it felt familiar to have a mother on loan. What a relief it was to know that someone, even a stranger, was taking care of us for a couple of days. All too soon we'd have only our stubbornness and our volatile love for each other to rely on when things got tough.

POETRY AND PREJUDICE

IF ONLY I had known what he was going to say when he stood up, I would have stopped him. But how? *Don't read your poem out loud, Brad—you have no idea of the effect it will have on me?* Or, as I had said every other morning: Please hand your papers up to me and I'll read a few of them aloud? That had worked fine for the first four class meetings. I had been able to screen out the worst of the blood and gore. I had read the hunting poems with their slitting of throats, removal of scalps, antlers, ears, and eyes, and their dragging out of guts. But I hadn't read the poems in which the throats being slit were human. As a criterion for selection, I have some doubts about this now, but I had to think on my feet those mornings, leafing through a sheaf of unappetizing poems.

It was the mid-eighties, and I was the poet-in-residence at Joseph High School, in the shadow of Oregon's Wallowa Mountains near the Idaho border. This first-period class consisted of twelve seniors—and I didn't like them. Unlike all the classes I had worked with the previous week, this one had not responded to any of my attempts to interest them in poetry. With only one more day, I had begun to think it wasn't going to happen. This frustrated me. Always before I had managed to make a good connection with my students.

Earlier that morning I had driven, as I did every day before school, down the road from my borrowed cabin on Wallowa Lake towards Joseph, where I had worked several times as a visiting poet. I loved this part of the state. It had become one of those rare, special places where I could relax into the beauty of the landscape and work on my own writing in the quiet hours after school—one of those places that imprints its colors and its contours on my mind forever. Each time I had completed a residency here, I'd angled for return invitations, which, so far, had always been forthcoming.

As I approached the Nez Perce burial ground, I turned for a last look at snow-covered Chief Joseph Mountain, paying deliberate attention to the shadows playing across the surface of the lake, on which patches of ice still floated in the shady spots. I didn't want to grow too accustomed to this breathtakingly beautiful place; I wanted to be amazed, every day, that this was my drive to work. Along the side of the lake, deer lifted their heads from the grass, which was faded and limp where it had just emerged from the snow, and turned their huge, dished ears my way, while I wondered how to connect with this unusually difficult group of students—wondered how to like them better.

They didn't like me either. It wasn't hard to tell. The ten boys overflowed from chairs and desks, long legs in skin-tight blue jeans sprawled forward with the pointed toes of their cowboy boots sticking up defiantly, as if giving me the finger. The two girls giggled together and never finished writing anything, but screwed up their papers and threw them away in loud disgust, as if to reassure the boys over and over that they had appropriately low expectations of themselves. At first, seeing how outnumbered they were, I had felt sorry for them, but by now I was exasperated. Of course, I had encountered all these common teenage behaviors in other classes at other schools, but I had usually managed to bypass the careful indifference of the kids and find something that excited them, however reluctant they were to show it.

Brad, for instance, seemed like other teenagers I had known: intent on looking cool at all costs, but underneath perhaps more interested in the poems than he let on. He was the tall one who always sat in the back left corner of the room. His jeans were so tight they must have impeded both movement and circulation, but he tried, not very successfully, to imitate the relaxed style of someone who was both comfortable and self-confident. Underneath the studied pose, he seemed pensive; often he stared out of the windows behind me, his expression so wistful that I turned to look outside too: the line of snow-covered peaks stood out like cardboard cutouts against the brilliant blue sky. It was stunning. But what did Brad see, I wondered. Was he thinking about being out there on the slopes? About hunting? His poems this week had described the thrill of early-morning stalking; a twig snapping underfoot; a doe's eye in the sights of his gun.

If only I had known what he was going to say when he stood up, I would have planned my response the way I carefully, obsessively, planned it later—after the event, when it was too late. "Bigotry," I would have written in large letters on the blackboard, and I would have started with racism, which surely these students already knew was frowned upon, at least in some circles. What they heard at home, of course, might be another matter. Most of them, I imagined, were not exposed to progressive views. Indeed, I had just heard about a lawsuit filed against Wallowa Lodge, the old hotel up at the lake, which had refused accommodation to a woman with a multiracial child. Later I heard that she won her case and got some damages, but still the incident told me something about how impervious many people here were to the moral standards that had finally been written into law—how free they felt, not only to hold on to their prejudice, but also to act on it in a public and visible way.

Back then, it was an isolated community, rife with tension between the long-term inhabitants, most of whom were loggers and ranchers, and the new, many of whom were artists, writers, and reclusive intellectuals, enjoying the beauty and peace of what had come to be called the "Little Switzerland" of Oregon. The isolation was beginning to break down, whether the old-timers liked it or not, as hikers came in to climb the mountains, llama trekking became fashionable, and—most controversial of all—the old sewer system that had polluted Wallowa Lake was replaced by a new one, which would allow for the development of more summer homes. It's not hard to imagine how what must have seemed like an invasion to some got translated into various prejudices in the privacy of my students' homes—variations on the "Jews, commies, and queers" theme. But I had never thought about any of this until Brad read his poem that morning.

The teacher, Dan, was sitting at the back of the room. I had talked to him a couple of times about this unresponsive group, and he had been concerned. Dan hadn't given up like so many of the teachers I had met in my frequent visits to schools around the state: he communicated his excitement about literature; he wrote poems for my classroom assignments, which he shared with the group; and he coached the students in reading dramatically, which some of them enjoyed. But nothing had made much of a dent with this class.

That morning, I started by handing out a William Stafford poem, which we read aloud. In "Serving with Gideon," Stafford describes a moment of decision he faced when he had to throw in his lot with the "good old white boys" of his town or take a stand against them, in Kansas during the segregated thirties. In the poem, the young Stafford deliberately carries his Coke from the drugstore and goes to stand with the Black elevator man, who is not allowed to drink at the counter—a small act, perhaps, but a very large decision. As we talked about the poem, I was aware that this group probably had limited ability to empathize with the Black man—and perhaps not even with the young white man troubled by racism—but I figured that, a few weeks away from graduation, they might know what it felt like to face important choices.

"Write a poem about an important decision in *your* life," I suggested.

For the next ten minutes there was a lot of squirming, writing, balling up of paper, and giggling. I tried to write too, as I always do, using my own assignments to generate lines or images that I might use later.

But I found it hard to concentrate in the atmosphere, which was any-thing but peaceful. The two girls, who were sitting in front, whispered to each other until I stared at them, when they pouted and looked at their paper, but made it clear they were just waiting till I turned away so they could resume their conversation. A couple of boys were reading paperbacks, which I decided to let go, since they were at least being quiet. Brad was staring out at the mountains again and I found myself speculating about his thoughts. In one of his hunting poems, he had come close to lyricism as he described the aromatic smell of the pines and the breeze humming and sighing at that moment before he fired. Was this dreamy smile caused by his recollection of the deer looking up at him as he softly squeezed the trigger?

I checked my watch. Another five minutes was all they would manage.

I knew Brad's father had taught him to hunt. He had written about that yesterday, though he refused to read the poem aloud. Learning to hunt was part of learning to be a man up here—I understood that, just as I understood that reading a poem aloud was a definite challenge to that tenuous manhood. Yet many of these kids would get out of Wallowa County as fast as they could. The smart ones would be off to college or to jobs in the city, where some of the others would find only unemployment and trouble. Few wanted to farm or cut trees like their fathers, and hunting deer would be no passport to manhood in their new lives. For all I knew, Brad was dreaming about high life in the city. Staring out at the spectacular scenery, which he had seen his whole life, maybe he saw, instead, the skyscrapers of New York and himself—all decked out in his suede jacket with the fringes swaying to the rhythm of his stride, swaggering into some dive where everyone looked up through smoke and saxophone vibes to admire his entrance.

I checked my watch again, and asked, "Anyone want to read a poem?"

Brad leapt to his feet, once again a six-foot-two-inch cowboy, his face reverting to its habitual smirk. His poem, he announced, was called "On a Mission." Gesturing melodramatically with his arm, he declaimed:

> Once on the mountaintop
> I heard a voice say
> "You can be a Hero
> if you choose, and this is how.
> Go out and find all the gays
> and kill them. You will be
> a Hero, praised by the whole world."
> I had to decide.
> I don't want to remain
> obscure.
> So I made my decision:
> I got my gun and began my task.

As he finished, bowing low from the waist, the room erupted into wild guffaws and applause. Sitting on a high stool up front, I watched as the laughter seemed to take over, sweeping wildly around the room, seizing them all, even the girls, until they were in the grip of some emotion that had nothing to do with humor. For once utterly satisfied to be who they were, they laughed until tears glistened on their flushed faces.

It took a while for it to dawn on them that I was sitting very still on my stool, not laughing, that my cheeks were bright red, although I have no idea what expression my face registered as I struggled to keep control of myself. Inside, my body registered hot fury. It was *me* Brad wanted to kill—but I was afraid to say so, and while the laughter whirled around the room like a tornado, I sat at its center, my heart drumming in my ears, my mind turning over and over like an engine that won't fire.

The first thought that came into my head was that if I told them I was a lesbian I would not be physically safe in the cabin. There was no phone there and I was one of only a handful of inhabitants up at the lake this early in the season. I could already see the pickup truck full of rowdy boys with a couple of guns in the rack, hurtling down the track in the dark; I imagined the headlights penetrating the living room windows as it swung on to the grass in front of the cabin. I knew how their big, competent hands would hold the knives and guns they had been writing about all week. Then it flashed through my mind that there would be other repercussions: in this contract work, which I relied on for a significant part of my income, it would be easy to phase me out—I wouldn't have to be fired; I just wouldn't get invited back to any of the schools up here when word got around.

It certainly wasn't my first confrontation with homophobia, yet it entered my body in a way that was different from anything I had encountered before. As the laughter tore around me, it was as if the outrage I had politely suppressed throughout my life was suddenly unlocked. It heated me up from the inside. Indignation, a sense of injustice, and the kind of frustration that makes you want to be a baby, yelling and waving your fists, all pulsed through my bloodstream. I felt hot enough to explode.

If only I had known what he was going to say when he stood up, I would have gathered up my courage as I have done so often when preparing to take that leap off the cliff, but probably, even then, I wouldn't have said the words, "I am a lesbian." It's true that I wasn't physically safe up there alone in that cabin, and it's true that I would probably have lost all or part of my school work, but it's also true that I was just plain afraid of revealing myself in that room. I had no sense of being able to bridge the huge chasm between me and those twelve kids—no belief that my simple, true statement would reach them through the bubble of camaraderie inside which they floated.

Perhaps if we had already established a good relationship, I could have done it, could have gambled that whatever tenuous liking for me they had would withstand the shock of the revelation—that they would somehow incorporate my being a lesbian into an already established picture of me as a real person. But it wasn't like that. I had no rapport in the bank, no goodwill savings to draw on at this moment. Then, my thoughts jumped back to when, at the age of twenty, I was sitting at an outdoor café in Spain with a group of Spanish boys, all of them my friends. They were talking about a soldier, whose body had been found on the road to the army camp outside the town where we lived. The body, they said, had been left to rot, picked at by crows and other scavengers. I remembered the wave of fear I felt as the boys muttered the word *maricón*, ("faggot"), almost unable to say it aloud. I remembered the murmur of the café as I sat there blushing. And the sultry heat of that evening touched my skin again now, the smell of car exhaust rolling back over the years in great, noxious waves, as I remembered, most clearly of all, how much I wanted to cry out, but how I did not know what words would leap from my mouth if I did.

I sat quite still in the classroom until the laughter had died away and the students were uncomfortable with my silence. As it grew quiet, brief eruptions of congratulation broke out again, as one or other of them tried to prolong the shared pleasure.

"Hey, man, great poem!" said one, and a ripple of agreement ran round the room, like an aftershock.

"Right on Brad!" said another, accompanied by murmurs of "Yeah, yeah!"

But they couldn't keep it up as they glanced sideways at me, puzzled by my red face.

At the back of the room Dan was poring over some papers with his head down. I could tell he was scared by what was happening and it didn't seem as if he intended to help me out. I struggled to make a plan, but my body was buzzing, almost as if I were touching a low voltage electric fence, and my mind refused to follow a normal sequence of thought. It would formulate the first few words of a declaration intended to change the lives of these students, but then it would jump sideways, derailed by an incongruous memory, or by the words I should have said on some other occasion. I was talking in my mind to family, friends, strangers on buses, politicians. I was sitting in my brother's oak-paneled dining room as his wife described the women at her tennis club as a bunch of dykes. I was watching myself smile complicitly as my family sneered at the woman only I knew was my lover. I was on a stone terrace overlooking the Mediterranean, my heart tearing inside my ribs as the man with the gold tooth smoothly flirted with the woman I loved, and she responded to this stranger as if she were available so that no one would suspect us.

"I want to tell you something," I said finally, my voice shaking and higher pitched than usual. I grasped the sides of the stool with sweaty hands, willing myself to look casual, but terrified I might burst into tears. As I adopted what felt like an unconvincingly nonchalant pose, it flashed through my mind that I was doing with my body exactly what Brad did with his: trying to convince the class I was invulnerable, unshaken and unshakeable. I was trying to be cool.

"It is a known fact," I said, "statistically proven, that about ten percent of every population, no matter where it is, is gay."

There was a lot of shifting around. Someone muttered "dirty queers."

"So what?" said someone else, defiantly.

I paid no attention but waited until the uncomfortable silence returned. "There are twelve of you here in this room," I continued. "Statistics would indicate that at least one of you will turn out to be gay."

I paused as another, much louder wave of discomfort ran round the room, and I heard the words "No way, man!" surface from the scared babble. For a moment, it seemed as if the room might not contain the emotion that was packing the air. But still I took my time.

"A great many gay teenagers die by suicide," I said, "because of attitudes like yours. I hope that won't happen to anyone here." I paused and looked at them deliberately. "If it does, you will bear a terrible responsibility."

It was impersonal, stern, and just the kind of lecturing I had always ignored from old people when I was seventeen. But it was the best I could manage, and I was grateful to change the subject without losing all my equilibrium. I turned decisively to the side of the room furthest from Brad's seat and asked, "Anyone else want to read a poem?"

MY FIRST few years living in Oregon were marked by an enormous sense of culture gap. I explored the area, taking long hikes in the Cascades, visiting the high desert, the Malheur Wildlife Refuge, and other beautiful and remote areas unlike anywhere I had seen before. On these trips, I would pass through small towns that looked to me more like movie sets than places people actually lived. Joseph was like that, with its wide main street heading up from the valley, mountains off to the right and the left, and the red, wooden hotel with its swinging doors, its boardwalk, and its hitching posts, looking for all the world as if the Lone Ranger or Wyatt Earp might come swaggering out under the "Saloon" sign at any minute.

Who knows how long it would have taken me to put down real roots here if I had continued taking hikes and car trips, stopping at cafés for home-baked pies, and chatting with storekeepers? It was the Arts in Education program that allowed me to go out and live in my adopted state, instead of cruising through it, a perpetual tourist.

I started with a six-week stint up the Columbia River in Hermiston, where I learned a lot about potatoes, irrigation, and the amazing number and diversity of churches that could thrive in that community. Then, in Toledo, a mill town near the coast, where I lived with the science teacher's family for a couple of weeks, I watched what happens to kids when the mill closes, parents are out of work, and tensions at home skyrocket. It was the only school where the teachers' room had a combination lock on the door to protect their lunches in the refrigerator. Later, in Yamhill, set among rolling hills and vineyards, I witnessed the warmth and hospitality of the town as well as the determination of parents in an impoverished school district to get what they wanted for their children. There I was greeted with a message of welcome on the signboard outside the school, and then invited to buy a candy bar from a bin in the front hall to help pay for my residency.

Over the years, I became an Oregonian. I met enough people who were more recent transplants than I to start feeling like an old-timer. In Portland, I made friends, became part of various arts groups, taught classes at a number of colleges, and slowly, over time, came to feel at home. I learned to love this city that grew more sophisticated each year yet retained its endearing ability to imitate a village from time to time. What other city's population would turn out the way Portlanders did when the magnificent statue of Portlandia, created for the new city office building, floated up the Columbia on her stately barge? Where else would a tightrope walker dance across a wire to open the new Performing Arts Center, the streets below packed solid with well-wishers? And while I let Portland work its magic on me, gradually I found acceptance and support for my work as a teacher and writer, as well as for my life as a lesbian in a committed partnership.

But, as I visited schools in central and eastern Oregon or at the coast, schools in rural communities up mountains, in forests, or lost in vast tracts of high desert, I found myself prevaricating when a teacher asked about my poetry books.

"I'm sure your bookstore will be able to order them," I would say, knowing that the books would not arrive until after I left. And, although I always carry a few copies of my books when I travel around giving readings, I never offered them to the schools I visited.

There were, however, almost always a few parents and teachers like Dan, who had bothered to read my work ahead of time and were comfortable with the fact that my lesbian identity shone through some of the poems. I latched on to these friendly souls with gratitude, never, until the incident in Joseph, fully aware of how nervous I was in their communities. I rarely contradicted the widespread assumption that I was heterosexual.

My greatest ambivalence about this deception came up around the kids, not the adults. In question-and-answer sessions, the students asked me all kinds of things about being a poet and, inevitably, sooner or later one of them would ask, "Are you married?"

"No," I would say. "But I used to be."

This was true but misleading. I could tell they saw me as a woman alone. No children. No husband. It was hardly an accurate picture of my life in which Ruth and I had been together for more than a decade. I hated this lie—hated that it deprived the students of seeing the true diversity among us—hated that it withheld a model from some kid who would one day need it.

RIGHT AFTER Brad read his poem that day, I had a free period, during which I fled down the road and sat in the café behind the bookstore in Enterprise with a cup of tea, my hands still shaking. I told Mary, the bookstore owner, what had happened. She listened, murmuring sympathetically, and then gave me one of her homemade muffins. She didn't seem quite able to understand the extremity of my distress, which is not surprising since I didn't understand it myself. I went back to school and got through the rest of my classes with little enthusiasm for the poems, but warmed by the genuine thanks of the students I was working with for the last time.

Before I left school that afternoon, Dan came to find me and steered me into his classroom.

"I talked with Brad about what happened in class," he said awkwardly.

"Oh, yes?" I said.

"Brad was confused. He saw how angry you were, but he didn't understand why."

Dan shifted uncomfortably and I sensed he wanted to apologize for his failure to help me in the classroom, but I didn't want his apology.

I knew he couldn't afford to risk his job, which, unlike mine, was permanent.

"So what did you tell him?" I asked.

"I suggested that he talk to you about it. And I told him that bigotry was unacceptable, no matter what he heard other people say. He seemed startled when I said 'bigotry' and then he said he couldn't talk to you because he was going away and wouldn't be back till Monday, by which time you'll be gone."

"Oh," I said. And then, rather ungraciously, "Thanks."

I was still pretty angry at Brad as I drove around the lake to my cabin. I parked and went for a walk through the silent resort, past the pack station and a couple of closed motels. The late afternoon sun lit up the top of the mountains but left me in the shade, where heaps of icy snow still huddled under the pines. Groups of deer, their ribs standing out after the hard winter, looked up as I walked by, then returned to munching on the hay someone had put out for them. As the sun dipped behind the mountaintop, I turned back towards the cabin, thinking about Brad's confusion. How could he not know why I was angry? Could he really believe it would be an act of heroism to kill all the gays in the world?

Later, as I sat by the embers of my fire, the night a deep well outside the windows, my head nodded and my book fell from my hand. The occasional crackles from the fire faded as I fell asleep and found myself inside a dream. I was up on Chief Joseph Mountain, crouched under a clump of salal. Far below, the lake glinted, but I barely noticed it, so intently was I listening. I felt my scalp tighten as I slowly turned my head, trying to scoop the sounds out of the air into the hollows of my ears. As my face revolved, I noted the direction of the breeze by its cool touch on my cheek and I strained to hear the minute sounds which the breeze carried away and flung out into the valley.

In the dream, I did not know who I was. For a while the soldiers were after me, my brothers having followed Chief Joseph down the canyon towards Imnaha, while I hid up at the timberline, separated from them and vulnerable. Down the gorge were arroyos in which they would be able to hide: the soldiers, though many, were stupid when it came to rocks. They saw nothing. Then I became a deer. I felt my ears stand up on my head, clarifying and magnifying the chitter of a chipmunk far off to my left. I felt my nostrils flare. I felt my heart beat. And then, somehow, I was human again, my clumsy feet unsure on the shale, my ears failing to identify the one sound that mattered—the crack of the twig under Brad's boot. When I heard the metallic click of the gun, I knew it was too late.

I woke sweating in spite of the freezing temperature. My breath condensed in a cloud as I rubbed my eyes and switched on lights to dispel the power of the dream. Wrapping myself in a sleeping bag, I reflected on my role here in Wallowa County. However temporary I might be, I was a member of this community; teachers and parents had welcomed me, lent me a cabin, and invited me to their homes for dinner. I had come here with a certain amount of respect already granted me by virtue of their school's invitation. And yet I had contributed to this community's intellectual isolation by hiding the truth about myself.

Remembering how much at home I had felt on my many visits here, and yet how cautiously I had behaved, I wondered if my unwillingness to trust the people around me was a mark of my own prejudice. Had I been seeing this place through the lens that newcomers to the West so often bring with them: the Wild West of the movies? Was I unwilling to treat people here as full human beings?

As I clutched the quilt around me and stumbled into the kitchen to make tea, my head cleared: the people in this farming and logging community had a right to know who I was and what I thought. They deserved the complexity and fullness that people acquire when they stretch to embrace a greater human diversity than they have previously known. I went back to bed and fell asleep.

In the morning I woke full of relief and resolve—relief that the class and the residency were over and resolve to be braver next time. Perhaps

I would write a poem, like William Stafford's, reflecting on the important decision I had made. I would not forget the very real dangers I had felt, but I would speak out; I would be myself.

It was good to be back in the city where I felt for the most part safe and accepted. There were nights when I found myself having that conversation with Brad that had never happened—even nights when I considered going back to find him, so we could talk. I wondered if he might turn out to be just one more scared, gay young man. But the dream I had had that last night at Wallowa Lake stayed with me: I remembered the smell of that breeze and how it felt to sniff it for signs of the human predator. And Wallowa County stayed with me too, the extraordinary grandeur of its scenery etched into my mind and my poetry, while its people gradually came into focus. I struggled to stop seeing them as *the other*—they were, after all, no more a bunch of "redneck loggers" than I was a "commie queer."

ALLEGIANCES

MOST EXPATRIATE Britons I knew referred to the old country as "home," sometimes after living abroad for thirty or forty years and becoming a citizen of somewhere new. When they asked me about my next trip "home," I would refuse to collude with them and answer lightly, "My home is here now." Yet when I had been a permanent resident for several years and started thinking about becoming an American citizen, I was surprised and somewhat confused to discover myself more attached to being British than I would have thought.

I was glad to be living in the US; everything that was most important to me was here. But I still had bouts of missing England. I missed the smells of grass and sea; the silhouette of the downs I had grown up walking and riding across, the particularity of moorland, bogs, beech woods, and rolling farmland ploughed and planted for centuries. My attachment to the primroses and cuckoos of an English spring, to the patterns of tile and brick on Sussex cottages, and to the proportions of country lanes with dense hedges barely skimming both sides of my car, remained stronger than my attachment to British people as a group, or even to their style of conversation, which I had found difficult to let go of, so firmly entrenched had it once been.

It was a sensual thing that embraced farmyard smells, the shape of kissing gates, and the patterns of shadows racing across sheep-shorn hills. I even missed the pebbles on Brighton Beach that made a barefoot walk down to the edge of the sea such an ordeal, and the vicious winds that lashed the Undercliff Walk in winter, hurling shingle up against the wall of white chalk.

Some people don't have to be attached geographically in order to identify with a community: historically the Jews are a great example of a people who look to the group, rather than the ground they live on, for that sense of belonging. But my own heritage is very different: never without a place to call their own, my ancestors were rooted for generations in places I know intimately. When I was a child, my mother walked with me through Banstead churchyard where her people, the Lamberts, lay under old beech and oak trees, their names engraved on tilting, moss-covered gravestones reaching back hundreds of years.

DURING MY years here, American culture has enjoyed peaks of popularity in Europe, but still, when I return to Britain, I find remnants of the old anti-Americanism that was rampant when I was a child. My parents, who were fairly typical of middle-class people in the fifties, considered Americans to be loud, ostentatious, and sometimes downright rude. When we went on holiday to Spain, we would often find American military families, stationed in Germany, staying at our hotel. Their cars were unnecessarily long with an excess of chrome that my father considered flashy; their children ran wild around the dining room and, according to my mother, had no manners whatsoever; worse still, the adults talked loudly about money, which was simply vulgar.

My generation, though, was enchanted with the cool American imports that were invading our TV stations with westerns and police dramas, and our radios with new rock and roll, pop hits, and classical jazz. High Street stores attempted, but failed, to capture the aroma of true hamburgers, but were more successful at producing the blue jeans that were growing in popularity; nevertheless, we, too, weren't above badmouthing Americans.

By the time I was considering citizenship, I had begun to look at things British with an equally jaundiced eye: the absurdity of the royals; the tawdry tabloids; tediously stereotypical Miss Marple and her ilk. These were not newly acquired perspectives, but they'd become more tiresome.

At this point, I had been with Ruth for nine years, and early on we'd settled the matter of where we would live. Ruth had made it clear that she couldn't live in England. She had grown up among Jewish immigrants from Europe after World War II, her father easily identified as a foreigner by his accent and loose grip on American idioms. She had seen what it took to learn a whole new way of interacting with others—the subtle clues that are second nature in your own culture, but hard to acquire in a new one.

I, too, had probably inherited my feelings about living in a foreign country from my parents. Mine had lived for more than a decade in Barcelona until the Spanish Civil War sent them fleeing back to England; in Spain they were part of an expatriate community, still British, even while living abroad in a cosmopolitan city.

Perhaps because my mother's happiest years were in Spain, after my parents died in the early sixties, I spent three years living there myself. I had a job as a tour guide at Perelada Castle and wine cellars and lived in nearby Figueres, then a small market town. Living in another country offered me a refuge, an escape. But, of course, neither my parents nor I were stateless refugees: we could return to England whenever we chose. Given that I was amenable to living in another country again, and Ruth's ambivalence, we made our home here.

LIVING IN America was one thing; becoming an American was something else. There were plenty of rational reasons to do it, the most compelling being that, although I was here legally, I had no vote. In fact, I could vote neither in the US, where I was resident, nor in the UK, where I was a nonresident citizen. This state of disenfranchisement felt morally wrong and was frustrating. I was volunteering on political campaigns of all kinds, sending checks to candidates and to support (or oppose) ballot measures, but when election day came around, I couldn't cast a vote. In the eighties and nineties in Oregon, it was particularly painful to have no say in the outcome of anti-gay ballot measures, for which I wrote op-eds for the major newspaper, canvassed door to door, and drove around on election day for the Democrats collecting last-minute ballots.

I distrusted nationalism and regularly voiced my skepticism of it. "As American as apple pie" had been the banner under which women campaigned for something in the eighties (was it fairness in women's sports or equal pay?) and I had voiced my objection. Justice is important for its own sake, I had claimed; we shouldn't appeal to knee-jerk chauvinism; that unthinking emotion leads to all kinds of injuries and to wars. (I hadn't reckoned on the power of the apple pie on feminists. The slogan stayed.) But if I was so opposed to nationalism, how could my own nationality really matter? I couldn't explain it satisfactorily, even to myself. All I knew was that my Britishness, even though barely a trace of English accent remained, was a part of how I saw myself. Without it, I would be less attached to my place in the world. Less myself.

In the end it was not the logical arguments that sent me to the immigration office to pick up my naturalization handbook. It was, rather, a slow, cautious putting down of roots into the soil. This same body that responded to a Welsh drystone wall started responding to a sagebrush desert; my eye became accustomed to the proportions of canyons and mile-wide rivers. I found in myself the capacity to love more, and different, geographies, which turned out to be a matter not of replacement but of expansion.

THE NATURALIZATION ceremony was held in the Bonneville Power Administration auditorium. We about-to-be-new citizens were seated in the center portion of the hall, over a hundred of us. Ruth, and our good friends, Ursula and Charles, sat in the side section among many who were poised with video cameras to record the moment when their loved ones would walk to the front and receive their certificates, stamped with a gold seal, admitting them to membership of one of the most sought-after clubs in the world. As we filed into our seats, volunteers at the end of each row handed out tiny paper stars and stripes, which we held by their wooden stems, as if they were lollipops. We all sat, eyeing one another, some, perhaps like me, trying to guess our neighbors' origins, or perhaps, unlike me, waiting nervously for the moment when we would be safe from *La Migra*. Then the volunteers hooked ropes across the ends of the aisles and stood guard by the exit doors as if we might all suddenly change our minds and make a dash for it.

I was sitting between a man who looked Vietnamese and a young woman from Central America, or possibly Mexico. Her knees were shaking as she folded her hands around her flag and looked down, trying to shrink into her seat; I tried to think of something reassuring I could say to her, but thought that my sudden voice, even a whisper, might give her a jolt. Looking around, I realized that I was one of only three Caucasians. This moment must have been, for most of the others, the pinnacle of years' work. Even if they had already dealt with the disillusionment or shock of a first encounter with American racism, some of them were experiencing this day as a salvation from violence or poverty, an escape from brutal, day-to-day tyranny, a chance at the thing we call liberty. As a woman I've experienced discrimination and as a lesbian I've struggled against the pernicious effects of homophobia, which I would never minimize in the range of human sufferings, yet I could hardly look at the United States as my refuge. It was just as rampant with the prejudices that threatened my personal safety and well-being as was Britain. I was not escaping anything: I had made a choice, first to come here and now to stay.

An immigration official came to the podium and asked us all to stand. Some of us rose to our feet immediately while others, like the man on my left, who had not understood, had to be nudged. Still clutching our flags, we looked towards the platform, a sea of dark heads—Southeast Asian, South American, Central American, Middle Eastern, and African—out of which rose three, including mine, taller than the rest. Our heads and shoulders seemed to sprout as lilies sprout from the dark leaves that lie flat and dense across a pond. In that company, for a moment, I thought about the great experiment—the ideals that, however flawed in practice, I had already made my own.

Raising our right hands, we recited a long oath, none of which I now remember except the part about renouncing "foreign princes and potentates," which made me want to laugh until I realized that there might be some who came from countries where the word "potentate" would not be out of place. We sat down to listen to another official tell us about our new country. He started with the glories of the physical geography: mountains, rivers, forests; the wheat fields of the Midwest and the great cities. I had no quarrel with this: we were pledging our allegiance not just to a vast society, but also to this particular piece of the earth. Then he told us that America was a country made great by immigrants, neatly skipping over those who were here when the first settlers arrived and throwing out the names of many who had come from other parts of the world to play an important role in the country's development—all of them white men. I sunk into an all-too-familiar rage at the obliteration of women and people of color and looked across to where Ruth was sitting: she was rolling her eyes and, when she saw me, shrugged and threw up her hands. My mind wandered as the man droned on until I heard him brazenly state: "This is a Christian country built on Christian principles."

I gazed across the hall again to where my people sat. They were looking at me with raised eyebrows, shaking their heads in disbelief. I was wondering how many of these new immigrants considered themselves Christians; I certainly didn't: I was—and am—an atheist, also a part of Ruth's Jewish family, and fully aware on both counts of how this man's sentence was a slap in the face.

The exits were still blocked and until we held that all-important certificate in our hands, it wasn't safe for anyone to start an argument, not even me, the loud-mouthed lesbian-feminist who had marched and lobbied, defaced billboards, and was rarely afraid to speak up.

Turning back to the stage, I caught the conclusion of the dismal speech. Americans, we were being told, were guaranteed "Life, liberty, and the pursuit of property."

We hurried up, one at a time, flag in hand, some striding purposefully, others almost tiptoeing, to receive our piece of paper, but it wasn't quite over yet. The exits remained guarded while children from the Harriet Tubman Elementary School took the stage. Lined up in their best clothes (one obviously wearing her mother's hat), twenty-five second-graders sang a selection of songs, accompanied by their teacher at the piano. "America the Beautiful" was delivered with gusto, though not always on key, and "The Star-Spangled Banner" made several of my near neighbors cry. Then, as the children ran down the steps from the stage, the ropes at the end of the aisles were unhooked, and all of us new Americans surged out, dazed and relieved. Some walked quickly to leave the building as if they didn't fully believe they were safe yet.

"Christian country indeed!" exclaimed my group all the way through the lobby and down the street. Charles, a professor of French history was amused by "Life, liberty, and the pursuit of property," as that was John Locke's phrasing—although Locke hadn't meant property in a narrow sense; Jefferson, as everyone knows, had chosen "happiness" instead. Surely an immigration official should be expected to know that most famous line in the Declaration of Independence. We agreed that it was appalling.

Ruth couldn't let go of the "Christian country." "What bullshit," she said loudly, unconcerned that others could overhear. "We have no established religion." Hearing it said in an official context in 1994 occasioned only outrage, not apprehension. We thought the guy was stupid or possibly an evangelical nut. We couldn't have imagined, back then, that Christian nationalism would surge during our lifetimes, would take over state legislatures, make inroads even into the Supreme Court.

By the time we reached home, we had hatched a plan. Ruth called the Jewish Federation, which immediately went into action, and I called our congressperson. A few weeks later, we heard that the welcome speech had been modified; the Christians and property were both out; happiness was back in. But we never heard about who would henceforth be included in that list of exemplary immigrants.

That night we gave a party to celebrate my new status. There was champagne and beer, laughter and reminiscence. Ruth had ordered a large cake, decorated with the words of that staunch anti-nationalist, Virginia Woolf: "As a woman, I have no country. As a woman, my country is the whole world." In the middle of the dining table, on the left side of the cake, I put a miniature Union Jack; on the right, the Stars and Stripes. My plan was to burn both during the course of the evening. When the moment came, I took the flags, sprinkled them with lighter fluid, and put a match to them, but they jointly refused to make the statement of a satisfactory blaze. Instead, being made of something unknown to the natural world, they spewed black smoke and shriveled into sticky globs.

A FEW weeks later, a large, shallow box arrived by special delivery. I sliced through the tape and eased the lid off. White paper covered something stiff and canvassy, and there, neatly folded to the exact size of the box, lay a flag.

I might not immediately have recognized that it was a flag had it not been for the certificate, printed on yellowish, pseudo-parchment paper bearing an image of the White House. On each side was a flag, the one on the left showing a circle of thirteen stars, the one on the right bearing fifty. In case I missed the point, large blue type between them announced "The Flag of the United States of America." As I carried the box into the house, I read the typewritten message: "This is to certify that the accompanying flag was flown over the United States Capitol on April 29, 1994, at the request of the Honorable Elizabeth Furse, Member of Congress." Then, "This flag was flown for Judith Barrington on the occasion of becoming a US citizen."

It was hard to believe that Congress had any reason to celebrate my citizenship until I learned from our good friend Phyllis, who worked for Congresswoman Furse and had been responsible for the gift, that members of Congress fly flags for all kinds of people, to acknowledge their red-letter days. After the flying, some person whose job it is to dispatch flags to worthy citizens, sends along the very item (or so they say) that waved in the Washington breeze. My flag looked, to my suspicious eye, far too pristine—crisp folds and an absence of smuts or wrinkles—to have ascended the flagpole, even in sunshine. I later learned that such flags are raised and lowered all day.

Once again, cynicism jostled with appreciation until it struck me that I had been given the perfect metaphor for my becoming an American. Richard Nixon had died a few days earlier and flags had been ordered to be flown at half-staff for a month. My flag had snapped joyfully in the wind halfway between the lowest point of the pole and the crown.

I found myself fingering the edge of the white canvas and wondering if it was burnable.

WHAT THE LIVING DO

IF YOU'VE never had reason to visit the North Front Cemetery in Gibraltar (and why should you?), you might find it hard to imagine how it sprawls across hard flat ground with that famous wedge of rock jutting into the clear blue sky, watching over the strategic strait to the south and over the dead to the north. At its foot lie Catholics, Protestants, Jews, and nothing-in-particulars, all taking an eternal sun bath beneath this piece of British soil just eight miles from Africa. There, too, lie my mother and father.

I don't claim to have made a comprehensive survey of cemeteries, but I have visited quite a variety. I like wandering where the spirits of the dead linger and, in fact, just three blocks from my house in Portland, Oregon, is a beautiful graveyard. My dog used to love it as much as I do; we spent happy hours there together, I reading names that now belong to city streets as well as to early pioneers, and she gamboling among the old firs and maples, dodging between headstones with her tongue hanging to her knees, sprinting after squirrels that scurried up trees to spit their squirrelly curses down on her head. Together, we wandered among the Wetherbees and the Birrells, turned past chipped urns and carved stone trees, our bodies breaking the pearly spider-webs that stretched between granite markers and the iron bars of a mausoleum; sometimes our feet and paws stepped accidentally on the slabs naming Viola Cadonau and her Patricia, who died at three days old. But that was before the "No Dogs" sign went up and the place began to be patrolled by groundskeepers.

In New Orleans I discovered that the dead lie, not discreetly underground, but overhead in massive tombs. In Mexico, I visited Patzcuaro, where the dead lie on an island in the lake, and on the Day of the Dead, festive, singing people row through the reeds and across the water, while the music of guitars and trumpets echoes around the shore as night falls, the lanterns and candles on the island merging with the galaxy overhead. In London, I wandered through Highgate Cemetery, giving a passing nod to Christina Rossetti, Radclyffe Hall, and Karl and Eleanor Marx.

To one who grew up by the blousy bluebell woods and smooth-flanked downs of Sussex, nothing will ever quite equal an old English churchyard. Indeed, I've never been able to shake off a certain regret that my parents do not lie near daffodils, under chestnut trees, in a graveyard filled with crooked stones and birdsong. Though they were infrequent churchgoers, the square Norman tower of the church, the lychgate, and the local woman coming in to do the flowers would have been comfortably familiar. But like so many who are buried at Gibraltar, their final resting place was dictated by the sea.

There are two cemeteries in Gibraltar. The better known one is the Trafalgar, named for the casualties of the 1805 battle in which Admiral Lord Nelson was killed. Nelson, however, was not buried at Gibraltar; only two sailors who died in that battle are there. The North Front Cemetery, much larger than the Trafalgar, also has its share of maritime victims. John Trust Curtis, age fifty-two, chief officer of the S.S. *Sidoh*, in February 1883 fell overboard and drowned. More recently drowned, and arguably less careless, is a group of those who died when the Greek Line's *Lakonia*, midway through a Christmas cruise, caught fire near the Canary Isles in 1963. One hundred and twenty-eight bodies were picked up by rescue ships and taken to Gibraltar, where many were buried, though some were transported to their home countries. A handful of Germans (*Johann Feichtenschlager*) and a few Greek crew members (*Doannis Roussos*) lie scattered around Section C, where the British majority also rests: *Marjorie Spurgeon, Clara Bate, Joyce Potter*, and, in plot number 3140, *Reginald and Violet Barrington*.

WHEN I first went to Gibraltar, nine months after the cruise came to its tragic end, I had just turned twenty. I was working for the summer in Spain and my older sister, Ruth, flew out to Barcelona to meet me. Our parents had been buried with a temporary marker; our mission was to arrange for a permanent headstone.

After I picked Ruth up at the airport, we drove into the center of the city where we settled at an outdoor café on the Ramblas and spread a map of Spain across the white iron tabletop. Clearly, she was shocked to see how far it was from Barcelona to Gibraltar—some five hundred miles on what would turn out to be a narrow, two-lane road choked with cars, donkey carts, and noxious trucks, trailing blue exhaust.

What might have been a sort of pilgrimage to the symbol of our greatest loss was more like a reprise of the few years, long before, when we had lived at home together. As we drove down the coast, we stopped to spend nights in Tarragona, Cullera, and Lorca. In the mornings we sang old songs and ate grapes and melon until we were sticky with juice and, in the afternoons when we got too hot in the open-top car, we stopped to run down a beach and plunge into the sea.

We arrived in Gibraltar late, after a particularly long, hot drive along the Costa del Sol. Ruth had an angry burn on the side of her neck and her left arm, where the sun had caught her as I drove west in my English, right-hand-drive car. We never discussed, on that day or any other, what we would do when we arrived, nor, indeed, did we so much as mention our dead parents. It was almost as if we were working hard to forget that they'd died, even while taking care of the business of their deaths. Memory on hold, I would spend years in a kind of oblivion, even when much later I wanted to recapture my mother and father. It would be years before I met people who were unafraid to talk about them and longer still before I tiptoed reluctantly out of forgetfulness. Grieving would unlock the box inside which those dead parents were waiting.

Strange as it seems now, we acted like two sisters enjoying a carefree holiday, which is perhaps why we were so startled when Gibraltar appeared, we crossed the frontier, and checked ourselves into the Queen's Hotel. I remember that next day only as a short series of photographic images. There was my first glimpse of the cemetery, much emptier than it is now, with wide expanses of white ground between clumps of graves, each religion with its own section. Then a cluster of black, wooden crosses named for *Lakonia* victims. I gazed at those temporary crosses, thinking, as I had thought the previous January at the memorial service, *this is a big thing . . . I really ought to be crying,* but those emotions eluded me. I had spent the last nine months keeping them on hold, drinking all night, dancing in bars, having complicated romances, and staying perpetually on the move. Somewhere behind those frantic distractions, I knew that if I stayed still and quiet for more than an hour or two, something awful would happen—something that I was nowhere near ready to cope with.

Two more images remain: the dark office where my sister made the engraving arrangements with the oily-haired cemetery manager and then, in late afternoon heat, a path high up on the Rock where notices warned us to hold on to our belongings and mangy apes held out their wrinkled palms for treats.

The only genuine feeling I can recall is the shock that jolted my whole body when we drove to the airport to find out when Ruth, who had a standby ticket, would be able to fly back to England. There was room on the very next flight, which would leave in two hours! We rushed back to the hotel, collected her suitcase, and then I found myself standing breathless in the small airport terminal watching her plane tear down the runway that crosses the isthmus connecting Gibraltar to Spain. Just when it seemed the plane would run right off the end of the tarmac into the ocean, it lifted off and climbed steeply into the twilight. I had never before felt so alone.

I had no choice but to stay on in the room at the Queen's Hotel, which that night contained one very empty twin bed. The next morning I was off again, speeding along with the top down, heading for Granada.

I DIDN'T return until 1987. In the twenty-three years since I'd been there, my parents' remains had been moved, a stone marker had been erected, and the appearance of the cemetery had vastly changed.

With me this time was another Ruth—not my sister, but my sweetheart and life partner. Without her, I would never have thought of going back; indeed, my family had no history or tradition that I knew of involving visits to the dead. But Ruth always visited her mother's grave when she was nearby and, to her, it seemed perfectly normal that I should do the same, even though I was by then living some seven thousand miles away.

Over the years I watched as Ruth's family observed the traditional Jewish customs that are so well tailored to the natural human reactions following a death. When first her mother, then her father, died, I could see what a relief it was to have a structure laid out ahead of time for the bereaved as well as for their family and friends. I often wished that my brother and sister and I had had such rituals to help us as we muddled through, hardly allowing our grief any public expression.

It was October when Ruth and I made that same drive from Barcelona and rented an apartment for two months high up in the old Moorish village of Salobreña, with views across bright green fields of sugarcane to the Mediterranean; in the afternoon, waves rolled across the tall fronds as the wind stirred up patterns that repeated in the blue sea beyond.

There, we settled into daily life, writing and reading, getting to know our neighbors, and shopping in the square where a few farmers displayed their produce and half a dozen fishermen sold their daily catch for an hour each morning. Then, one day, we set out from Salobreña for our foray into Gibraltar and found our way to the cemetery.

I have written about that second visit, both in poems and in my memoir, *Lifesaving*: how Ruth and I went to the office, where the manager, Mr. Sanchez, ran a finger down the list of names, the writing spidery and the ink a faded blue, in a black ledger straight out of a Dickens novel. I wrote, too about how we searched and searched, under the searing sun, for the grave and how I was haunted by Mr. Sanchez's casual words when we persuaded him to help us; standing helplessly near a sprawling patch of blackberries, he shrugged and gestured towards the bushes. "Could well be under there," he had said over his shoulder, as he hurried back to the shade of his shack.

After that we covered our heads with newspapers and spare shirts and sat in despair on a wooden bench next to a hibiscus bush, but, in a sudden moment of confidence, I walked straight to the stone that was broken and lying on its face in the weeds. It was Ruth who realized that the visit could not be salvaged—we were too exhausted and overheated—and suggested that we return a few weeks later.

She encouraged me to write down what I might want to say at the graveside, a sort of address to the parents who had died before I had a chance to know them as an adult. As I walked in the afternoons around the village, or on the headland jutting into the sea, I mulled this over and made notes on the pad I carried in my shorts' pocket. I didn't want to plead for acceptance, nor did I want to apologize; I knew they would have had a hard time understanding why I had chosen to follow a precarious living as a writer and to live my life as a lesbian, but I needed to trust that, had they lived, we would have found a way through the difficulties. I dredged up all the dignity and pride I could and outlined the life I had created far away in Oregon: the writing and teaching; the interesting and challenging blend of cultures, landscapes, and languages that permeated my daily existence; and my relationship with Ruth around which everything else was built.

Five weeks later, when I sat on the ledge that outlined the grave next to my parents, it was pleasantly hot. I thought about what a sun worshiper my mother had been—how every summer she had reclined in a deck chair in the back garden until she turned nut-brown and how she had walked for hours around town when we were on holiday in Spain, more energetic in the midday sun than she ever was in the gray months of an English winter. And I remembered my father on those holidays: his Panama hat with the black band; his thin white legs on the beach; the sunburn that reddened his shoulders and balding head. For a moment, in this hot place a stone's throw from Africa, I could almost hear my mother scolding him still: "For goodness' sake stay under the sunshade, Rex!"

The calm trilling of the cicadas sounded like Spain, not England, as did the distant clanking of construction outside the east wall—the ubiquitous background noise of coastal towns around the Mediterranean. Occasionally, one of the large seagulls that circled the Rock would swoop down and cross the cemetery with a plaintive cry as if suddenly remembering to pay tribute to the dead. It was one such cry—a mewing that seemed to have gathered all the heartache that had ever risen from this place—which moved me from pleasant reveries into a bleakness that was as close to sorrow as I had yet come.

I lit the candle I had brought and dropped it into a jar. On the stump of the broken headstone it burned steadily, offering a kind of hypnotic comfort as I focused on its flickering, which was all that was visible in the glaring sunlight. Then I placed four stones and a hibiscus bloom on the grave, unfolded my notes, and began to speak in a low voice about my life. When I was finished and had grown quiet again, the air seemed neither hostile nor laudatory; it was just profoundly still. I put the notes back in my pocket and was surprised to find tears running down my face. It felt good to sit there and cry quietly, almost peacefully, until the candle burned out.

Before we left, we went to find Mr. Sanchez to see about mending the stone. He assured us that the local stonemason would smooth off the jagged edge and make sure that the grave was well finished and clearly marked. I handed him a wad of notes, wondering if it would go straight into his pocket, and warned him untruthfully that we would be back soon to look at the repairs. We had no plans to return.

IN THE spring of 2006, I was invited to teach a writing class at a lovely arts center in the mountains near Alicante. It was Ruth who again urged me to plan a visit to my parents' grave and she who accompanied me when, after the workshop was over, we made our way via Granada and Nerja to Málaga, stopping along the way to look with resignation at the new developments along Salobreña's beachfront.

The once-tedious drive from Málaga through Torremolinos and Fuengirola, Marbella and Estepona, had become a fast but expensive trip along the new *autopista*. We arrived at the main gate just as a large funeral procession emerged from the nearby chapel and proceeded with halting steps and muffled sobs into the cemetery. A young woman, popular in the community, had died suddenly; the benches that lined the covered entrance were piled high with wreaths.

Once again, we were struck by fierce heat as we stepped into the North Front Cemetery, which looked disconcertingly different from how we remembered it. In the nineteen years since we were there, the cemetery had grown crowded; the different religions no longer had separate sections and, with all the infilling, the dead mingled ecumenically. Standing near the gate was a new director, more businesslike than Sanchez, but too busy with the funeral to help us. A groundskeeper in a sweat-stained T-shirt walked with us towards Section C, pointing out the tall fir that marked its beginning and stating with confidence that all the *Lakonia* victims were buried near the east wall.

I had thought it would be easy to remember the location of the grave, but it wasn't. The lay of the land was unrecognizable, full of new markers, some of which stood on a flat-topped hill that had not existed before. The only thing I felt sure about was that, no matter what the groundskeeper said, my parents were not buried near a wall.

The mournful tones of the priest conducting the burial nearby added to our mounting despair when we realized that, once again, we were searching under a scorching sun for a grave that was not marked on any map. A helpful secretary was able to locate the plot number, but in true Spanish fashion—British soil notwithstanding—the plot numbers turned out to bear no relationship at all to their location.

Ruth had been smitten with an acute allergy attack and was popping Benadryl in the shade of the fir tree. The burial was over and the mourners, enveloped in a throbbing cloud of melancholy, were drifting past us, the older women leaning on younger men whose faces registered bewilderment.

"We've covered the whole of Section C," Ruth said, trying not to sound worried.

"You don't remember it being near the wall, do you?" I asked.

"No, I don't think so," she said between sneezes and wheezes. "But maybe we should look there."

Ruth went off in the direction of the wall and I walked on down the path until I came to a wooden bench that seemed like the one we had sat on years earlier. Indeed, it was next to a tall bush that might well have been a hibiscus, though without the flowers I couldn't be sure. Still, I was struck with the same sudden confidence that had struck me before. I stepped off the path into an overgrown area where this time there were no blackberries; weeds and wildflowers bloomed in a riot of spring colors: pink convolvulus, yellow buttercups, tall purple weeds I did not recognize, and gorgeous scarlet poppies nodding their perfect heads. My feet caught in the tangled undergrowth and tripped on the rims of ancient graves, but there in the midst of the cheerful blooms, partly obscured by foliage, I found the low stone marker, its mended top squared off and its face blotched with patches of lichen. Near the bottom, under my parents' names, the writing was faint but legible: "Lost at Sea, December, 1963."

I felt no need, this time, to talk about myself or seek parental approval; it was no longer a matter of any importance that my parents give me and my life their blessing. The three visits I had made were in no way a substitute for the regular conversations, weekend gatherings, bitter arguments, or shared pleasures that mark an evolving relationship with living parents. But I'd learned, through those trips to Gibraltar, what, perhaps, others learn much earlier about visiting the dead. My parents had become real to me, and I was able to have a chat with them precisely because I was there at their very tangible resting place. I would certainly never have done it sitting in an armchair at home.

Of course, those few trips to Gibraltar, decades apart, were not by any means the only times when I felt myself move along in my relationship with my parents. But it was something about sitting by the grave that allowed me to turn aside from the deep rut of the familiar and step out in new directions. Each time I was there, something shifted; first I'd acknowledged the particular loneliness of living without parents since the age of nineteen and then I'd been able to look past my abandonment and comprehend their nightmare experience. Now I was left only with an appreciation for the people they had been.

Ruth settled on her shady tomb and pulled out a copy of the poem I had written after our previous visit—a poem describing the frustrating search for the grave and expressing certainty that I would never return. I had intended to read it there, but finding myself close to tears, I asked her, instead, to read it aloud. When she came to the end, we both cried and then, after a few minutes, smiled: we had returned after all.

For a while we sat there: no construction noise this time, but still the ubiquitous cicadas. A red admiral butterfly trembled in the air over the headstone, the white spots near its wingtips brilliant against the black of its upper body, and the red band across its forewings catching the light. It seemed in no hurry to move on—indeed, it appeared to be offering something, perhaps just a few minutes of bright companionship.

In some cultures, people believe butterflies to be the spirits of the dead returning, and in seventeenth-century Ireland, killing a white butterfly was prohibited since it was believed to be the soul of a dead child. For a moment I wondered if this butterfly was a visiting soul: one of my long dead parents? Or perhaps our recently dead, beloved dog, come back to offer us comfort. But the ledge beneath my thighs was too rock-solid, the air too suffused with the salty breeze and the perfume of wildflowers for my thoughts to stray to a world I didn't believe in, out of sight, beyond this hard-baked earth. If the souls of the dead were anywhere, they were surely right beside me in the petals of the convolvulus and the smooth granite of this and every gravestone in every cemetery around the world. The dead had no need to hitch a ride with a butterfly; the red admiral's spirit was all its own.

YEARS EARLIER when we visited Mary Wollstonecraft's grave, it was the warm, rough surface of her stone pressed into our backs that insisted she had once been more than history, more than legend, more, even, than the brave, wise words for which she is famous; she had been flesh and blood—a live woman who might at any moment come striding through the buttercups in her long skirt and boots, throwing back her head and laughing.

I wonder now if a grave is any different from other memorials. Certainly, our visits to Virginia Woolf's Monk's House, Radclyffe Hall's White Cottage, and Barbara Hepworth's home and studio in St Ives all resembled our visit to the St Pancras churchyard in that they added a new dimension to our sense of those remarkable women. Yet graveyards seem to offer their own, uniquely profound moments. In the last few years I have seen the orderly graves standing to attention in Normandy, the rose-covered gateway to a churchyard on the

Isle of Wight, and the windswept graveyard in the slate-gray village of Heptonstall, Yorkshire, where Sylvia Plath lies beneath unruly bouquets and passionate notes. In each of these places people come to carry on a relationship that was snatched from them by illness, accident, war, despair, or the slow weathering of time that finally felled the one they loved. Such a place has a power that draws us and that power occasionally ignites a spark between the living and the dead.

It is possible that a grave is especially powerful because it houses the bones of the dead. People have speculated that elephants create their own graveyards, leaving the herd and seeking, when they are about to die, a place that is special precisely because many elephant bones lie there. And, of course, in many human cultures, burial sites and the bones of the dead are sacred. But what Ruth and I didn't know, when we leaned against Mary Wollstonecraft's stone and felt her presence so strongly, was that her bones had long since been moved to Bournemouth, where she and her husband, William Godwin, were reburied beside their daughter, Mary Shelley.

It's true that I thought about my mother's crumbling bones when I sat under the shadow of the Rock, conjuring up her living presence. But I hope that underground scapulas and tibias and worm-infested skulls are not essential to communing with the dead, since, for all kinds of reasons, I believe in cremation. What matters most is surely the existence of a special place where one can talk to the dead; where what is unfinished can, over time, become more resolved; where the living continue to grow and the dead do whatever it is the dead do.

ACKNOWLEDGMENTS

THESE SHORT memoirs were written over decades. I wish to thank the editors of the literary journals that first published some of them, often in an earlier version and with a different title: *Creative Nonfiction; Catamaran; Mary, A Journal of New Writing; Harvard Gay & Lesbian Review; Junctures; Alligator Juniper; 1966: A Journal of Creative Nonfiction; The Chattahoochee Review; ZYZZYVA*; and *Narrative Magazine*.

Thanks also to the editors of the anthologies that first published two of these memoirs in earlier versions: *Hers3: Brilliant New Fiction by Lesbian Writers*, Terry Wolverton and Robert Drake, eds., Faber and Faber; and *The Stories That Shape Us: Contemporary Women Write About the West*, Teresa Jordan and James Hepworth, eds., W.W. Norton.

Many of these memoirs were written in whole or part at Cottages at Hedgebrook, The Tyrone Guthrie Centre, Residencies at Centrum, Sitka Center for Art and Ecology, Caldera Artists in Residence, Atlantic Center for the Arts, and the Writers Room at the Multnomah County Library.

After a brief visit to Jeanette Winterson's café in London, I spent a delightful afternoon at The Women's Library (previously The Fawcett Library), home of an archive of the history of UK feminism from the late nineteenth century to the present day. I was delighted to discover a comprehensive collection of Women's Liberation Newsletters from the seventies—the very same ones that I had typed and run off on the unpredictable mimeo machine.

Pablo Conrad of the Adrienne Rich Literary Estate generously allowed me to quote from unpublished letters written to me by Adrienne Rich.

I had a fine time working with Kim Hogeland, Micki Reaman, and Tom Booth at the excellent OSU Press. I am grateful to Kim for selecting *Virginia's Apple*, to Micki for her intelligent and creative editing, and to Tom for so skillfully keeping all the plates in the air with great good humor. Katherine White arrived just in time to help *Virginia's Apple* find its audience.

Several writer friends helped me as I revised and edited these memoirs. Tricia Snell read the whole manuscript and gave me abundant wise feedback. Joanne Mulcahy, Sandra Williams, and Jackleen de la Harpe each offered insightful comments on a new piece that I wrote to add to the collection.

Conversations about writing with friends have been important to me, especially those with: Maxine Kumin, Adrienne Rich, Mimi Khalvati, Janice Gould, Grace Paley, John Morrison, Valerie Miner, Zack Rogow, Ursula K. Le Guin, Andrea Carlisle, Paul Merchant, Peggy Shumaker, Evelyn C. White, Judith Arcana, and Barbara Sjoholm.

Ruth Gundle, in addition to plucking the eponymous fruit, has shared with me a family of friends and relations, and a daily life, for forty-five years. I am more grateful than I can possibly say for each of those years and for all she does to make our life together rich in interest and physically manageable in the face of my disability. Her brilliance as an editor helped me to work these memoirs into a collection. She has always been my first and best reader.

CREDITS

Imagine

Page 70. "Freedom's just another word for nothin' left to lose." Excerpt from "Me and Bobby McGee" by Kris Kristofferson, recorded by Janis Joplin in 1970 for the album *Nightbirds*. Copyright © 1969 by Kris Kristofferson.

Westering

Page 126. "*Voulez-vous coucher avec moi ce soir?*" Excerpt from "Lady Marmalade" by Bob Crewe and Kenny Nolan, recorded by Labelle, in 1974 for the album *Pearl*. Copyright © 1974 by Bob Crewe and Kenny Nolan.

Page 127. "Hey! Mr. Tambourine Man . . . " Excerpt from "Mr. Tambourine Man" by Bob Dylan. Copyright 1964, 1965 by Warner Bros. Inc.; renewed 1992, 1993 by Special Rider Music.

Wild Patience

Page 146. "What would happen if one woman told the truth about her life? / The world would split open." Excerpt from "Käthe Kollwitz" by Muriel Ruyekser, in *The Collected Poems of Muriel Rukeyser*. Copyright © 2006 by Muriel Rukeyser. (University of Pittsburgh Press, 2006)

Page 146. "No one ever told us we had to study our lives / make of our lives a study, as if learning natural history / or music . . ." and ". . . We cut the wires / find ourselves in free-fall, as if / our true home were the undimensional / solitudes, the rift / in the Great Nebula." Excerpts from "Transcendental Etude" by Adrienne Rich in *The Dream of a Common*

Page 148. ". . . because your face has been looking at me all year from our SW office wall." *Excerpt from an unpublished letter by Adrienne Rich to Judith Barrington, December 15, 1981, copyright © The Adrienne Rich Literary Estate, 2023.* Reprinted with the permission of The Adrienne Rich Literary Estate.

Page 151. "I still feel warmed and exhilarated by the flow of talk we were all able to have during my stay in Portland—how I hope we can do it again before too long!" *Excerpt from an unpublished letter by Adrienne Rich to Judith Barrington, February 27, 1982, copyright © The Adrienne Rich Literary Estate, 2023.* Reprinted with the permission of The Adrienne Rich Literary Estate.

Page 154. ". . . the skin these hands will also salve." Excerpt from "Integrity," in *A Wild Patience Has Taken Me This Far: Poems 1978–1981* by Adrienne Rich. Copyright © 1981 by Adrienne Rich. (W.W. Norton and Company, Inc., 1981)

Page 154. "I returned home in better shape than I left, and your hospitality (space, talk, food, drink, hot tubs) had much to do with it." *Excerpt from an unpublished letter by Adrienne Rich to Judith Barrington, February 27, 1982, copyright © The Adrienne Rich Literary Estate, 2023.* Reprinted with the permission of The Adrienne Rich Literary Estate.

Page 155. "I do hope to get at least a look at you both." *Excerpt from an unpublished letter by Adrienne Rich to Judith Barrington, January 9, 1986, copyright © The Adrienne Rich Literary Estate, 2023.* Reprinted with the permission of The Adrienne Rich Literary Estate.

Page 155. "The longer I live the more I mistrust / theatricality, the false glamour cast / by performance." Excerpt from "Transcendental Etude" by Adrienne Rich in *The Dream of a Common Language: Poems 1974–1977* by Adrienne Rich. Copyright © 1978 W.W. Norton and Company, Inc. (W.W. Norton and Company, Inc., 1978)

Page 155. "It was extremely moving to me to hear the villanelles . . . I think your work will always have to address that event at its deepest core, and when you work with it directly, your strongest & most poignant writing comes forth. Not that I imagine that is easy or can be happening all the time. But you have shown that you have the courage to keep going back—& it will not be simply the rehearsing of old trauma & loss, it will grow in you in new ways, & in your writing." *Excerpt from an unpublished letter by Adrienne Rich to Judith Barrington (undated, marked "Feb. 1986" by Judith Barrington) copyright © The Adrienne Rich Literary Estate, 2023.* Reprinted with the permission of The Adrienne Rich Literary Estate.

Page 156. "I hope the enclosed doesn't look too forbidding to you. It's because I do care about what you're trying to do here that I took the time to think about what seems to me to hold the poems back, where that happens." *Excerpt from an unpublished letter by Adrienne Rich to Judith Barrington, July 24, 1986, copyright © The Adrienne Rich Literary Estate, 2023.* Reprinted with the permission of The Adrienne Rich Literary Estate.

Page 157. "You could so easily have settled to be a charming, witty lesbian poet, period, with these caverns and reaches untouched for fear of too much pain & foreboding." *Excerpt from an unpublished letter by Adrienne Rich to Judith Barrington (undated, marked "Feb. 1986" by Judith Barrington) copyright © The Adrienne Rich Literary Estate, 2023.* Reprinted with the permission of The Adrienne Rich Literary Estate.

Virginia's Apple
Page 177. Sappho fragment "You may forget . . ." From *Sappho: A New Translation* by Mary Barnard. Copyright © 1958, 2019 by the Regents of the University of California. (University of California Press, 2019)

ABOUT THE AUTHOR

JUDITH BARRINGTON's *Lifesaving: A Memoir* was the winner of the Lambda Book Award and was a finalist for the PEN/Martha Albrand Award for the Art of the Memoir. She is the author of the best-selling *Writing the Memoir: From Truth to Art*, widely used in creative writing programs, and five collections of poetry, most recently, *Long Love, New and Selected Poems*. Her work has appeared as one of *Creative Nonfiction*'s "Favorite Prizewinning Essays" and been included as notable literary nonfiction in *The Best American Essays*. She and her partner Ruth Gundle founded and ran The Flight of the Mind, a residential summer writing workshop for women that took place for eighteen years in the foothills of Oregon's Cascade Mountains. They were also founders of Soapstone: A Writing Retreat for Women, now Soapstone: Celebrating Women Writers. Judith was a faculty member of the University of Alaska, Anchorage MFA Program and has taught creative writing at universities and writing conferences across the US and the UK, as well as in Spain, Greece, and Mexico. She was born in Brighton, England, and lives in Portland, Oregon.